CRIME TIME
– AUSTRALIANS BEHAVING BADLY

Sue Bursztynski

Sue Bursztynski grew up in the beachside suburbs of Melbourne, where she still lives. For many years, she wrote fiction and non-fiction for small-press science fiction magazines before she won the Mary Grant Bruce Award for children's literature and realised that what she enjoyed most was writing for young people. She has written nine books, one of which, *Potions to Pulsars: Women doing science*, was a Notable Book in the Children's Book Council Awards. Another, *Starwalkers: Explorers of the unknown*, was nominated for the NSW Premier's History Award.

When not writing, Sue works in a school in Melbourne's western suburbs. She enjoys reading, music, handcraft and old science fiction movies.

Louise Prout

Louise is an artist and illustrator. She has published over 28 children's books and is currently illustrating the new Quentaris series.

Louise's mother taught her, at a very early age, how to draw and capture likeness, mainly in pencil, pen and watercolour.

In 1993-94 Louise's drawing career took off when she produced a best-selling calendar called 'Tall Poppy Target' Dartboard Calendar. This won the Australian Gift Award for that year. She then worked for sports magazines caricaturing celebrity personalities and politicians, before discovering and coming home to the delightful realm of children's book illustrations.

To Mum and Dad, Mary, Gary,
Maurice, Jo, David, Mark, Bianca
and all the younger members
of my terrific family

Also by Sue Bursztynski

Monsters and Creatures of the Night
Potions to Pulsars: Women Doing Science
Starwalkers: Explorers of the Unknown
It's True! Your Cat Could Be A Spy

CRIME TIME
– AUSTRALIANS BEHAVING BADLY

by
Sue Bursztynski

Illustrations by Louise Prout

FORD ST

First published by Ford Street Publishing, an imprint of
Hybrid Publishers, PO Box 52, Ormond VIC 3204

Melbourne Victoria Australia

Text © Sue Bursztynski 2009

Illustrations © Louise Prout 2009

2 4 6 8 10 9 7 5 3 1

First published 2009

National Library of Australia Cataloguing-in-
Publication data:

Crime Time – Australians behaving badly /
Sue Bursztynski

ISBN 9781876462765 (pbk.).

Target Audience: For children.

Subjects: Crime – Australia – Juvenile literature.
             Criminals – Australia – Juvenile literature.

Dewey Number: 364.10994

Cover design © Grant Gittus Graphics
In-house editor: Saralinda Turner

Printing and quality control in China by
Tingleman Pty Ltd

INTRODUCTION

This is *Crime Time*, so get ready to discover Australia's very own gallery of rogues – an Aussie litany of heinous crimes, dastardly deeds and terrifying tales…

The human race is extraordinarily diverse in its interests. Some people are captivated by shoes and clothes, some engrossed with football or cricket or snowboarding, some would never be parted from their music players and some cannot turn off their mobiles although their texting thumbs are weak with overuse. Yet everyone – whether it be reluctantly or eagerly – is fascinated by wicked misdeeds and illegal acts.

When I was a child my sisters and I would sneak looks at my father's paperback copy of *The Encyclopaedia of Murder* by Colin Wilson and Patricia Pitman. It was kept in his wardrobe and we had to creep into the room and sit on the floor, hidden by the creaking wardrobe door, to read those terrible tales of blood and slaughter, of Jack the Ripper and the cannibal Alexander Pearce. How we shuddered with delicious fear when Pearce said he preferred human flesh because it was far tastier than pork. And we would read on, shuddering, until we were caught, or until it started to get dark and we had to tiptoe down the long, dim corridor after reading about the betrayal and massacre of the crew of the *Batavia*.

These pleasures, these spine-juddering tales, are now laid out for you, and you don't even need to hide behind the groaning wardrobe door to read them.

Within these pages lie Pearce the cannibal and murderous Frederick Deeming, here is Sarah Makin with babies buried in her garden and there is Caroline Grills with her poisonous desserts. Here is a gallery of dreadful deeds and matchless crimes, from a well-planned caper that robbed a club full of bookies of all their cash to the sickening Snowtown murders with their ghastly barrels of human flesh. Here too, are the shamelessly audacious – like Lola Montez whose spirited attempt to find a spider in her dress left her nearly naked before an audience of Gold Rush miners.

In this book you may feed yourself on horrors. Murders for money. Murders for status or position, murders for respectability and even murders for fun…

But do not be afraid of dangerous strangers. Most murders in Australia are still carried out by family members. By fathers, mothers, lovers and children. Listen out for the knock on the window or the footsteps on the porch but listen harder for the beating of your own heart…

And now, get ready to unearth Australia's deep, dark history of crime, true crime…

Kerry Greenwood, Melbourne 2009

CONTENTS

20th Century:
1900s – 1930s:

1940s – 1950s:

1960s – 1970s:

1980s:

JERONIMUS CORNELISZ
THE 'BATAVIA' INCIDENT

In 1629, long before Captain Cook explored the east coast of Australia, a Dutch ship called *Batavia* arrived on the western coast. However, it wasn't exploring. It was wrecked.

Batavia was a beautiful ship on its first voyage. It was full of treasure, with soldiers and passengers on their way to Java, part of Indonesia. The captain, Ariaen Jacobsz, reported to the head merchant, Francisco Pelsaert. Third in command was a merchant called Jeronimus Cornelisz.

Cornelisz was a persuasive man who could talk people into doing things they would never normally do. He was about to do just this to a number of the crew.

One of the *Batavia*'s passengers was a beautiful woman called Lucretia van den Mylen. All three men found her attractive. Pelsaert was in charge, so he got to be nice to Lucretia. Jacobsz was jealous.

At the Cape of Good Hope, there was trouble over Lucretia, who had been attacked by some crew members. Pelsaert had to discipline them. Jacobsz was also still angry with him.

For this and other reasons, there was going to be a mutiny. Cornelisz would lead it. The crew would kill Pelsaert and the soldiers and take over the ship. Not only would they get all that treasure, they could turn *Batavia* into a pirate ship. And Cornelisz would get Lucretia.

But the ship was blown off course in a storm and ended up near the Abrolhos Islands, off the coast of Western Australia. On 4 June, *Batavia* crashed on a coral reef. The *Batavia* was breaking up so the passengers and crew had to abandon the ship. There were three islands nearby. Boats took the women and children ashore, while the crew packed whatever supplies they could.

Unfortunately, they made the mistake of leaving behind most of the water. On the islands, there was some food, but no water. Pelsaert and some of the crew took the last of the longboats to look for water on mainland Australia. In the end, they went all the way to Java, over 1000 kilometres away, because the coast was too rocky and steep to land.

While they were away, Cornelisz took over. The water supply ran out. Eventually, it rained, but several people had already died of thirst. Cornelisz didn't care. He had other plans. They would fix the ship. Those willing to sign an agreement with him to become pirates would live. Everyone else would die.

Cornelisz and his friends killed and killed, hacking people into pieces, drowning them, bashing them up. They murdered 125 men, women and children.

Meanwhile, a soldier called Wiebbe Hayes had led a small party of men to one of the other islands to look for water. They found it and sent a smoke signal up to let the others know. They had no idea what was happening on the big island until some men escaped the murderers and swam to their island.

Hayes knew he mustn't let Cornelisz win. He and his small group of soldiers prepared homemade weapons and set up a stockade from which they could fight. Cornelisz and some of his men rowed to the island, but weren't allowed to land. The battle went on for days. Hayes captured Cornelisz and some others.

On 17 September, Pelsaert returned with a rescue ship, *Sardam*. Hayes managed to reach it first, told his story and that was the end of the mutiny.

The mutineers were tortured for information. Some of them were taken back to Indonesia for trial, torture and execution. Others were executed right there, on the island, now called Batavia's Graveyard, starting with Cornelisz, whose hands were chopped off before he was hanged. Cornelisz showed no regret for what he'd done, crying 'Revenge!' as they hanged him.

Only two of the mutineers were spared. One was a cabin boy called Jan Pelgrom de Bye, the other a soldier, Wouter Looes. Instead of being executed, they were taken to the mainland and left there.

Nobody knows what happened to these two killers. Maybe they died, or perhaps they were lucky and were adopted by a local Aboriginal clan. Perhaps they even have descendants today.

DID YOU KNOW...?

Australia's youngest murderer was only seven years old. In 1908, Robert Davis of Irish Town, Tasmania, was arrested for the murder of his two younger brothers. However, when everyone realised how young he was, not even the prosecutor could bring himself to try a little boy and he was sent to a boys' home instead.

ALEXANDER 'CANNIBAL' PEARCE

When Alexander Pearce, an Irishman, was transported to Australia in 1819, it was for stealing a few pairs of shoes. Today, that crime would incur a small sentence, but in those days, it could get you hanged. Alexander, however, was lucky. He was sent for seven years to the penal colony in Van Diemen's Land (now Tasmania). In fact, some of Australia's nastiest prisons were in Tasmania.

Alexander went to Macquarie Harbour, a prison so tough that prisoners were willing to kill each other, just so they could go back to the Hobart jail for a break before they were hanged. At Macquarie Harbour you could be punished for the smallest things – even for singing! Prisoners worked for twelve hours a day in winter, sixteen in summer, on very little food.

Everyone believed that escape was impossible. The sea destroyed small boats, you couldn't swim to freedom and the bush around the settlement was thick. If, by some chance, you did get out, Hobart Town was 225 kilometres away.

In spite of all the risks, Alexander and seven other convicts decided to take their chances, first in a boat, then heading through the bush to Hobart Town.

One of the convicts, Robert Greenhill, was a former sailor and knew how to find his way. The others were Matthew Travers, Alexander Dalton, Thomas Bodenham, William Kennely, John Mather and William 'Little' Brown.

They hacked their way through the bush, but after nine cold, wet days, they had run out of food. Two days later, Kennely joked that he was so hungry he could eat a man. Robert Greenhill said this was a great idea. Human flesh, he said, tasted like pork.

The first victim was Dalton. He had volunteered to whip other convicts back at Macquarie Harbour and wasn't popular. Greenhill hit him on the head while he was asleep. The body was divided up the next morning.

Brown and Kennely, fearing they might be next, returned to Macquarie Harbour. They made it back, but were so exhausted that both of them died anyway. At least they avoided being eaten!

The next victim was Bodenham, whose body was shared among the four survivors. Even though they saw kangaroos and emus, the runaways had nothing with which to hunt them, so Pearce, Greenhill and Travers attacked and killed Mather.

After a snake bit Travers, he made a very tasty meal for Pearce and Greenhill. Finally, Pearce took Greenhill's axe while he was asleep and killed him. Taking an arm and a thigh, he continued on through the bush. From there on he was lucky. He met a shepherd, Tom Triffet, who was also Irish and was only too happy to help an escaped Irish convict. And Pearce learned that he wasn't too far from Hobart Town.

A few days later, Pearce left with two bushrangers, but in January 1823, soldiers caught the three men. The two bushrangers were hanged, but not Alexander Pearce, who was sent back to Macquarie Harbour. He said he'd eaten the other runaways, but the police didn't believe such a crazy story.

Other convicts at Macquarie Harbour now admired Pearce, because he had proved it was possible to escape. He might have got away with his crimes if he hadn't developed a taste for human flesh. He escaped again, this time with a boy called

Thomas Cox, who ended up as dinner. Pearce was caught with bits of Cox in his pockets and the boy's body was in the bush nearby.

On 19 July 1824, Alexander Pearce went to the gallows, not at all sorry for what he had done. 'Man's flesh', he said, 'is delicious, far better than fish or pork'.

DID YOU KNOW...?

Until a few years ago, a loophole in taxation law allowed convicted Australian criminals to claim 'business' expenses, such as bullets, guns and other equipment needed in the practice of their criminal careers.

MATTHEW BRADY
THE GENTLEMAN BUSHRANGER

When Matthew Brady was hanged in May 1826, thousands of women cried. He wasn't exactly Robin Hood; if he gave to the poor, we've never heard about it. But he was good-looking and he had – well, *style*! Also, he was known for his courtesy to women and not killing without good cause. In fact, he only killed once and that man had deserved it. No, not quite Robin Hood, but close.

Matthew Brady started life in Australia in chains. We're not sure why. It may have been for theft, or, according to some versions of his story, for forgery. Whatever the reason, he was sentenced to seven years and left his home in Manchester, never to return.

In Hobart, Matthew became an assigned servant. This was a system by which free settlers applied to have convicts to work for them. He hated being a virtual slave and tried to escape several times. During

9

the first three years of his sentence, Matthew was whipped 350 times!

Finally, Matthew went to Macquarie Harbour, a penal colony on Tasmania's west coast. No one escaped from there. That was until Alexander Pearce and seven others managed it in 1822. Of course, only Alexander Pearce had actually survived the journey, because he ate the others. But now convicts knew escape was possible.

In June 1824, shortly before Alexander Pearce was hanged, Matthew and thirteen other convicts escaped in a whaleboat, with soldiers shooting at them. Luckily for them, one of the men had been a Royal Navy navigator. He steered the boat to a place called Derwent.

There, they stole weapons and food and went inland to a place which is now known as Brady's Lookout. It was safe. They lived there in hiding while they rode out to rob people. The gang became known as Brady's Bunch.

Matthew nearly died when a man called Thomas Kenton, who had been receiving their loot, betrayed him. Kenton and two soldiers hit him and tied him up. The soldiers went to fetch more men. While Kenton was out of the hut, Matthew managed to burn through his ropes and grab Kenton's gun.

He didn't kill Kenton then. Matthew didn't like killing. But Kenton lied about him, saying he had killed troopers. A year later, Matthew shot Kenton, as he was sneering that he knew Matthew didn't kill people.

When Governor Arthur offered a huge reward for his capture, Matthew put up his own poster outside the Royal Oak Inn, offering a reward for Arthur's capture.

Matthew's men were loyal. One of the gang whom Matthew had kicked out for trying to rape a woman was captured, but refused to betray Matthew, even though he was to be hanged.

Over the next year, however, the men were killed off one by one, till only a few were left. The reward offered for Matthew had tripled to 300 guineas, around $700, which was a huge amount in those days. He had to get away before someone decided it was worth betraying him.

In late 1825, Matthew sent a message to the governor. He wanted to get out of the colony. If he didn't, he'd capture an important settler, Richard Dry. But Arthur had done something Matthew didn't know about: he had planted a traitor in Brady's Bunch.

Matthew kept his word, capturing the whole house, with family and guests. He had a wonderful time and so did the women. He danced with them and sang for them at the piano. But a servant slipped out and brought soldiers to help. Matthew rode out with his men, wearing the hat of a Colonel Balfour, who had led the soldiers. It was typically cheeky, but this was his last success. He had been shot in the leg.

Governor Arthur's spy, a convict called Cohen, told the soldiers where the gang was hiding. Matthew escaped, but his wound was still bad. He was caught by a bounty hunter called John Batman, who was to found Melbourne several years later.

Lots of people signed a petition to save Matthew's life. It didn't help. He had caused too much trouble to be allowed to live. While he was in prison, his admirers sent him flowers, food and fan letters. On the way to the gallows, women threw flowers at him.

Matthew bowed to the sobbing crowd, then accepted his fate.

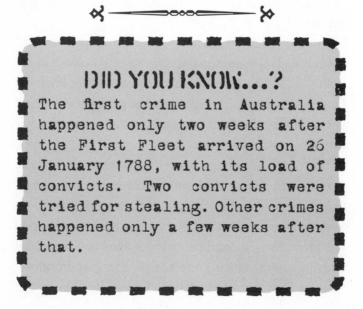

DID YOU KNOW...?

The first crime in Australia happened only two weeks after the First Fleet arrived on 26 January 1788, with its load of convicts. Two convicts were tried for stealing. Other crimes happened only a few weeks after that.

AUSTRALIA'S FIRST BANK ROBBERY

Sydney in 1828 was a very different place from today. Half the people living there were convicts. Not all convicts were kept locked up as prisoners are today. Many could walk around where they wanted as long as they went to work and turned up for church on Sunday mornings. Church was important. Any convict who didn't come to pray could be locked up.

While many people were sent to Australia for crimes that would get them only a fine today, there were others who just kept on doing things they shouldn't. The problem with keeping all those criminals in one place was that if anyone wanted to pull off a big heist it was easy enough to find experts.

James Dingle, who had been freed in 1827, had a wonderful idea. He knew about a drain under George Street, which led to the foundations of the new Bank of

Australia, where rich people kept their money. Why not dig through to the bank? He discussed the matter with a convict, George Farrell, and a man called Thomas Turner, who had been involved in building the bank. Turner gave some advice, but dropped out of the plan in case the police suspected him. The thieves replaced him with a man called Clayton. They invited a safecracker by the name of William Blackstone into their plot. If anyone could make this work, he could.

The robbers decided to dig over three Saturday nights. They couldn't do it on Sundays, because Farrell and Blackstone had to go to church, so they shovelled through the night. On the last Saturday, they were nearly through into the bank's vault, where the money was kept. They really didn't want to wait. So Dingle went to the convict supervision office and asked permission for Farrell and Blackstone to miss church that day. Whatever excuse he gave the clerk, it couldn't have been, 'They're busy digging into the bank vault'. Anyway, it worked and they kept digging until Sunday evening.

After a break for sleep, they went back and took absolutely everything kept in the bank. At about 2.30 a.m., they were coming up from the drain with their loot when two policemen came past. They spoke to Dingle, who wasn't carrying anything and told the officers that he had fallen asleep outside. One of the policemen was a little suspicious because it was a wet night and Dingle was too dry to have been sleeping out in the rain, but he let Dingle go.

On Monday, the robbery was discovered. A reward was offered for any information leading to the arrest of the robbers, but nobody came forward.

Now there was the problem of what to do with the loot. The bank notes were hard to spend, because the bank had records. The thieves decided to use a fence, someone who buys stolen goods and sells them to others. A fence called Woodward offered them a good price for the loot, then simply ran off with it. They did have some money left and they spent it gambling and drinking.

Blackstone was arrested for another crime and sent to Norfolk Island, a very nasty prison. He offered information about the robbery and Woodward, in return for freedom and a ticket back to England. The police agreed and in 1831 rounded up the other thieves. Dingle and Farrell were sentenced to ten years of hard labour. Woodward got fourteen years. We don't know what happened to Clayton, who wasn't arrested. Blackstone got his ticket home, but just couldn't resist stealing from a shop before he went. So much for going home. Blackstone was sentenced to life on Norfolk Island, but somehow managed to get back to Sydney.

However, somebody wasn't happy with him. In 1844, his body was found in a swamp in what is now the Sydney suburb of Woolloomooloo.

The Bank of Australia struggled on for several years after the robbery, but closed in 1843. The thieves had wiped it out.

DID YOU KNOW...?

Ikey Solomon was one convict who first came to Australia voluntarily. In 1827, Solomon was on trial for receiving stolen goods, but escaped while on his way back to prison: the coachman driving him there was his father-in-law! Solomon got as far as America, but when his wife, Ann, was sent to Tasmania for receiving stolen goods, Solomon went to join her. Everyone knew who he was, but he couldn't be arrested without the paperwork, which had to come from England. The arrest warrant finally arrived and he was sent back to England for the trial he'd escaped. Then he was transported - to Tasmania! The writer Charles Dickens, who saw his trial, wrote Solomon into his novel Oliver Twist as a villain called Fagin.

JOHN GILES PRICE
EVIL COMMANDANT OF NORFOLK SLAND

Today, Norfolk Island is a beautiful place with only a small population. To keep the island clean and unspoiled, the number of tourists is restricted.

In 1846, nobody wanted to go there. It was a prison for Australia's toughest convicts, the ones no other prison could break. The idea was that Norfolk Island would break them. It was in that year that Norfolk Island penal colony got the perfect Commandant.

John Giles Price looked like a kindly vicar. He was the sort of man you could imagine having a cup of tea at the church bazaar, chatting with old ladies about their gardens.

However, if you were a con- vict, you would find out very

quickly that you were wrong. Horribly wrong. John Price was a sadist, a person who enjoyed giving pain. He loved his job because it gave him huge power over others. It was said that even his wife and five children were terrified of him.

Flogging was a normal punishment in penal colonies. Sometimes those who did the flogging were convicts themselves. But John Price made sure that his floggers had training. He wanted to make sure that being whipped wasn't just something you had to put up with. You had to be terrified that it might happen to you. Convicts who had been beaten couldn't clean their wounds. Flies and maggots crawled all over them. And you could be flogged for anything. Talking back to a guard. Complaining. Helping a friend. Anything. Commandant Price wasn't fussy.

There were other punishments, of course. In one case, Price punished two men by putting extra time on their sentences. Their crime? One of them had shared food with the other. Prisoners were chained, beaten and gagged. One man who was in the hospital was chained to the floor for weeks because he had climbed to the window for fresh air.

In 1853, after several years of enjoying himself on Norfolk Island, John Price retired to a farm in Tasmania. If he'd stayed there, he might have lived to a ripe old age. But soon afterwards, he was offered a job as Inspector-General of prisons in Victoria and simply couldn't resist it. He accepted.

In 1857, he was at the prison hulks in Williamstown, Victoria. The hulks were ships used as cells. Prisoners went from there to work at the quarries nearby, but the cells were also useful to chain up convicts. You couldn't sit or stand properly in them and you might also be gagged. If you had a gag in your mouth, of course, you couldn't eat, which didn't stop the guards from throwing in bread and then taking it away, commenting that you obviously weren't hungry. When one convict protested about this to Price, the commandant ordered that the punishment should continue.

Finally, the convicts couldn't take it any more. They knew they would die for what they were going to do, but it seemed worth the price. One afternoon, when he was out in the quarries, the men attacked, trying to drag him to a tent made of bits of dismantled ship. There they had prepared a noose with which to hang him.

John Price was a strong man. He managed to break away from them and run. However, there were a hundred men around that quarry. As he tried to avoid the different gangs, someone managed to hit him with a heavy stone, knocking him over. After that, he was finished. The convicts hit him with anything they had in their hands at the time – hammers, stones, crowbars. There wasn't much left of him by the time they were finished, but he survived for another day before finally dying.

That was the end of John Giles Price. He had showed that you don't have to be on the wrong side of the law to be evil. Still, his memory lives on as the villain in Marcus Clarke's convict novel, *For The Term Of His Natural Life*.

DID YOU KNOW...?

Having a security system in your home isn't always much help, as some Melbourne gangsters found. When Alphonse Gangitano was murdered at home in 1998, the tape on his security camera was simply stolen. Charlie Hegyalji didn't have a tape in his camera at all. His home's front sensor light was broken on the night he was killed on his own doormat. The tall trees he had planted to make sure the police couldn't watch him made great cover for the killer.

LOLA MONTEZ

Lola Montez wasn't born in Australia. She didn't live here. But her tour of Australia in 1855-1856 made her a part of Australian legend.

Lola was born in Limerick, Ireland. Her real name was Maria Dolores Eliza Rosanna Gilbert. Lola Montez made a better stage name. She was very beautiful, with black hair and flashing blue eyes, and a lot of men found her irresistible, even though she had a scary temper.

By the time she arrived in Australia, she had been married several times and her boyfriends had included the composer Franz Liszt and King Ludwig of Bavaria (in what is now Germany). If she were alive today, she would be in all the gossip magazines, going out with Hollywood stars and millionaires.

Lola was a dancer. Not just any kind of dancer. You wouldn't see her in *Swan Lake* or *Sleeping Beauty*. Lola had created her very own dance, known as the Spider Dance. In it, she wore a gauze dress with spiders on it and the dance involved her trying to shake them off. Let's just say it didn't leave much to the imagination.

In 1855, the gold rush was on in Victoria, in Bendigo and Ballarat. Gold miners would like the Spider Dance, she decided. It had worked in

California, which also had a gold rush going on. She raised money, hired some actors and took her company to Sydney.

Lola got some good newspaper reviews in Sydney for her show, *Lola Montez in Bavaria*, but it was time to move on down south to Melbourne and then the goldfields, where all those rich miners were working. Lola decided to get rid of some of her company, which didn't make them happy. In fact, they sued her for damages. Someone from the sheriff's office in Sydney boarded her ship to demand the money she owed the sacked actors.

Lola went to her cabin and, soon after, sent out a message to say that she had taken off all her clothes, but the sheriff was welcome to come in if he liked. Of course, he didn't. Having got away with not paying, Lola continued on her way.

In Melbourne, Lola performed at the Theatre Royal, where her reviews weren't as good as in Sydney. She put up with the disappointment, even though the police banned her from doing a second performance. In Ballarat, however, she was furious with comments made by Henry Seekamp, editor of the *Ballarat Times*. She decided not to put up with this.

Lola caught up with him in the United States Hotel, where he was having an after-work drink, and beat him with a horsewhip. Seekamp fought back, but Lola won the fight and he had to run away. There's a saying that no publicity is bad publicity and this particular story, once it got around, gave Lola very good publicity. Tickets to her shows sold out and she was right about the miners. They threw gold nuggets on stage.

The show was just as successful in Bendigo and Lola also visited the goldfields themselves, where the miners adored her. They admired her courage and her willingness to go down into the deepest mine shafts.

Lola was probably glad she had visited Australia, because after she left, her life went downhill. She had had a wonderful tour, even with those people who had been shocked by her act and complained. After all, Lola was used to shocking people. She enjoyed it!

She only lived for five years after her visit to Australia, finally dying of syphilis in New York. Before that, she had found religion. It would be interesting to know how she felt about the Spider Dance by then.

DID YOU KNOW...?

In 1803, convict Joseph Samuels was condemned to hang for murder. Three times, the rope being used to hang him broke or unravelled, so he was allowed to live. It wasn't much help to him, though - soon afterwards, he drowned while trying to escape in a boat.

BRIDGET HURFORD

Bridget Hurford was a violent woman who terrified her husband, John, but when she decided he had to go, she made sure someone else killed him. This was a big mistake.

John Hurford, a farmer in the new colony of Western Australia, had made his fortune and when he decided, in his sixties, to settle down, he proposed to Bridget Larkin, a widow about half his age.

It seemed like a good idea at the time. Bridget had six children to support and in those days a woman couldn't simply put her children in day care and get a job. In 1851, the couple married and settled at Fishleigh Farm, near the coastal town of Busselton.

The marriage didn't work. Before the first year was out, neighbours were seeing them fight. Bridget even knocked out some of her husband's teeth. In early 1855, John Hurford told his neighbour, John Green, that Bridget had thrown him out and he needed somewhere to stay till he could move into a new home he had bought. Mr Green let him share a room with George Jones, one of the farm workers.

But in March, Mr Green had to ask John to move out due to lack of space. He had to move back to the farm. George had heard Bridget threaten to kill John a number of times. In fact, she had threatened to kill George as well. For John's safety, George agreed to share a room with him at the farm.

One day, John came home with a bad cold. Bridget pretended to feel sorry for him and sent him to bed with a hot drink. She told George that her husband felt so sick that he wanted to sleep by himself that night. After this, she made sure that her family and servants were either asleep or out of the house.

Then she found her boyfriend, a farmhand called Enoch Dodd, and ordered him to kill her husband. Enoch was frightened to do this, but he was even more afraid of Bridget. She gave him plenty of alcohol, to make him braver, and finally he went into the room where John Hurford lay asleep and strangled him.

Bridget told John Green and George Jones that she had found her husband dead. When George and another farmhand were preparing the body for burial the next day, they noticed a red mark on his neck. A policeman was called in.

A Dr Bryan examined the body, but didn't think the mark meant anything. He declared that John had died of natural causes. Someone found a will that put Bridget in charge of her husband's estate, although he had told George he would never leave her anything.

Bridget might have got away with the crime, but Enoch Dodd was nervous. He drank too much one night and talked. He told everything to a man called Philip Dixon, who also worked for Bridget. Enoch needed someone to tell his troubles to and Dixon seemed to be the right person because he was the one who had produced the fake will and wouldn't dare tell anyone.

Sooner or later all this talk was going to get out and it did. Bridget, Enoch and Philip were arrested and tried in October 1855. The whole sorry story came out. The so-called Dr Bryan, who had said John died of natural causes, turned out not to be a doctor at all. He didn't even know what you did with a stethoscope, the instrument doctors use to listen to a patient's heartbeat.

Philip Dixon was sentenced to life imprisonment in Van Diemen's Land (Tasmania). Enoch and Bridget were sentenced to death. Bridget believed she wouldn't be executed because she was a woman.

Bridget Hurford found out how wrong she was on 15 October. She became the first woman in Western Australia to be hanged.

'MAD' DAN MORGAN

The bushranger Dan Morgan was called Mad Dan because of his frightening mood swings. One minute he would be charming, the next he would lose his temper and shoot someone. The man was scary!

It's possible that he had a mental illness. We will never know.

Mad Dan was born John Fuller in New South Wales, 1830, the son of George Fuller and Mary Owen. When he was two, he was adopted by a man called John Roberts, who looked after him till he was seventeen. 'Dan Morgan' was just one of many aliases he took on during his life.

Dan worked as a stockman until 1854, when he left for the Castlemaine goldfields in Victoria. Perhaps he decided that robbing other people of their hard-earned money was easier than earning it himself, because he was soon breaking the law. He went to jail for armed robbery. He served only six years of his twelve-year sentence, released early for good behaviour, but Dan Morgan hadn't learned his lesson.

He returned to New South Wales. There, after a short time as a horse-breaker, Dan helped himself to a valuable horse. The horse's owner chased and shot him, wounding him. Morgan escaped to an area near the Victorian border, from which he could rob people in northern Victoria.

By mid-1863, Dan Morgan was a full-time bushranger. He committed many armed robberies. In August, he attacked a shepherd called Haley, whom he thought had informed on him. Haley survived the attack, but because of this, the New South Wales government put a 200 pounds reward on Morgan's head. It would be much bigger by the time he was killed.

The first murder we know for sure that he committed was of an innocent station overseer, John McLean. John worked on a station called Round Hill. In June 1864, Morgan came visiting. The terrified workers were rounded up. Morgan demanded rum. Now drunk, he accidentally shot at himself when he was about to ride off. Thinking someone else was attacking him, he threatened to kill the station manager, Sam Weston. However, he only shot Weston's hand, then ordered John McLean to ride for a doctor.

Suddenly it occurred to him that McLean might bring the police, so Morgan rode after him and shot him from behind.

Next, he killed a trooper called Maginnity, whose partner, Churchley, rode off and left him. Churchley was sacked for cowardice, but what he did is understandable. Anyone who had Mad Dan Morgan waving a gun at them wouldn't want to hang around. Other bushrangers had reasons for killing, but Dan Morgan might shoot someone just because it seemed like a good idea at the time.

The price on his head, which had already gone up to 500 pounds, doubled to 1000 pounds.

Morgan's next victim was a senior police sergeant called Thomas Smyth. He was killed in September 1864. By now Mad Dan's time was nearly up. He managed to commit plenty of robberies both in New South Wales and Victoria over the next few months, but his last hold-up happened on 8 April 1865.

Morgan raided Peechalba Station in Victoria. He held the family prisoner for the night. A nursemaid managed to escape. She warned the station's part-owner, Rutherford, who sent for the police from the nearby town of Wangaratta.

The next day, Morgan headed for the stockyards to choose a horse, taking three hostages with him.

The hostages weren't much use to him, as a station employee called John Wendlan shot him from behind.

That was the end of Mad Dan Morgan – but not of his body.

First a photo was taken of his corpse, posed with his gun. Souvenir-hunters cut off his beard and long, curly hair. His face was skinned. His head was sent to the professor of anatomy at Melbourne University to be cut up and examined. What was left of him was buried at Wangaratta Cemetery.

Today, people are still arguing whether Ned Kelly was a hero or a villain, but nobody thinks there was anything heroic about Dan Morgan.

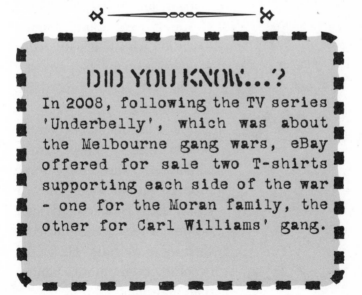

DID YOU KNOW...?

In 2008, following the TV series 'Underbelly', which was about the Melbourne gang wars, eBay offered for sale two T-shirts supporting each side of the war – one for the Moran family, the other for Carl Williams' gang.

FRANK GARDINER
AND THE EUGOWRA GOLD ROBBERY

In the 1860s, there was a gold rush in New South Wales, at Lambing Flat and Blackridge, near Forbes. Enough gold was being mined at Forbes to make it worth sending the treasure to Bathurst by coach every week. The coaches were escorted by armed guards, of course, but having a regular gold coach did make things easier for bushrangers.

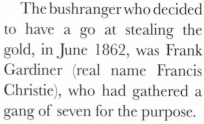

The bushranger who decided to have a go at stealing the gold, in June 1862, was Frank Gardiner (real name Francis Christie), who had gathered a gang of seven for the purpose.

Did the heist work? Well, yes – and no.

The gang members weren't professionals. They were cattlemen who did some robbery on the side. One of them, Ben Hall, would later become a full-time bushranger with his own gang. He would become even more famous than Gardiner.

Gardiner was a professional. On 15 June 1862, he and his gang held up some passing bullock drivers. He'd chosen a good spot, a gully called Eugowra Rocks, where the gold coach had to slow down, because the gully was steep and there were huge rocks to avoid.

Gardiner made sure that it was even harder for the coach. He parked the bullock drays across the road. One farmer had his young son, George Burgess, with him. George remembered the hold-up many years later, when he was the last survivor. The bullock drivers were not mistreated, though some were made to lie across the road. The rest were hidden and blindfolded.

As the stagecoach driver, Jack Fagan, was abusing the bullock drivers for getting in his way, Gardiner's gang leapt out, shooting and yelling, 'Bail up!' The horses reared. The coach tipped over on its side.

Nobody was paying Fagan and the four troopers with him to get killed, so they very sensibly ran off into the bush, towards Eugowra homestead.

The gang took money and gold from the coach. They released their prisoners and shared some drink from the coach. The delighted child, George Burgess, was given a pound – enough money, he wrote later, to make himself sick on lollies for two weeks!

It was the largest gold robbery in Australia's history. There was about $2 million worth of gold in today's money.

Unfortunately for Gardiner's gang, Jack Fagan and the troopers hadn't been wasting their time when they ran. They told the owner of Eugowra homestead, Hanbury Clements, what had happened. Clements rode off to Forbes to tell the police.

Constables, with the help of an Aboriginal tracker, managed to follow the bushrangers towards Gardiner's camp in Wheogo. The camp had a good view of the area, so the bushrangers could see who was coming.

They escaped, but really couldn't take all that gold on one horse, which was tired. Most of the gold had to be left behind. Gardiner and Ben Hall managed to hang on to their share of the treasure, but everyone else had to make do with the money.

Gardiner got as far as Queensland with his partner, Kitty. There, they lived at Apis Creek near Rockhampton, running a store till 1864, when a tip-off sent the police after him. He was arrested and sentenced to 32 years at hard labour, but he was lucky. His sisters appealed successfully and after only ten years in prison, Frank Gardiner was released.

There was only one condition: he had to leave Australia for good. As far as we know, he is the only Australian ever to be exiled.

Gardiner wasn't going to argue with a chance to be free. He went to Hong Kong for a while, then, in 1874, on to America. There, in San Francisco's Barbary Coast area, he settled down to life as a saloon keeper. He called his saloon the Twilight Star. He probably had children there – two of his American sons may have visited Australia in 1911.

We don't know for sure what happened to Gardiner himself, for in 1906 there was a destructive earthquake in San Francisco, which wiped out a lot of information about the later part of his life. But he probably died of pneumonia in 1904.

What happened to the gold? Did he spend it before he left Australia? Did he hide it? Did it come in handy in California?

We may never know.

DID YOU KNOW...?

If you were a woman in England in the early 1800s, you had to be very careful not to commit any crime. The population of the convict settlement in Australia was six men for every woman. In order to get some male/female balance and keep the men from going crazy, the British government changed laws to make it easier to transport women than men.

MARY ANN BUGG
SHE DID IT FOR LOVE

It has often been said that behind every great man is a great woman. Sometimes there has also been a great woman behind a criminal. And there is no doubt that the woman behind the bushranger Fred Ward, known as Captain Thunderbolt, was brave and strong and that he wouldn't have survived without her and her knowledge of the bush.

Mary Ann Bugg was born in New South Wales, the daughter of a former convict called James Bugg and an Aboriginal woman called Charlotte. Charlotte taught her daughter how to live in the bush. This knowledge helped Mary Ann and her husband survive when they were on the run.

When Mary Ann was ten, she was sent away to boarding school, where she learned to read and write and other things that young ladies were expected to know. By the time she was fourteen, Mary Ann had married her first husband, a shepherd called Edmund Baker. Mary Ann and Edmund went to live in a place called Mudgee, where they worked on a property owned by a lady called Mrs Garbutt.

Mrs Garbutt's son, James, had no problem about stealing other people's cattle and horses. His partner in crime was a cattle thief called Frederick Ward, the future Captain Thunderbolt. In 1856, the two men were caught receiving stolen horses and sentenced to ten years in Cockatoo Island prison. They ended up only serving four years before they were released. While they were in prison, Mary Ann's husband, Edmund Baker, died. When James and Frederick returned, Mary Ann was a widow with a young child. She had no reason to stay on the Garbutts' cattle station, so she left with Frederick.

Unfortunately, Frederick just couldn't stop stealing and in October 1861, he was back on Cockatoo Island for stealing horses, while Mary Ann gave birth to their first child, a little girl called Marina.

Mary Ann wasn't going to let her husband stay in prison any longer than she could help. She had to wait until she had finished breastfeeding her daughter, but then she left both children with someone who could look after them for a while. Mary

Ann got a job as a housemaid in Balmain, which was near Cockatoo Island. She was careful to use a false name, calling herself Louisa Mason.

The story goes that she swam to Cockatoo Island with a file, so that Frederick could use it to cut off his chains. Is it true? We don't know, but it's a good story. Regardless, Fred did escape in September 1863, and they moved to the Hunter Valley, where Fred's life as a bushranger began. Oh, and the children went with them. In fact, the couple had another one. Captain Thunderbolt never really had a gang. Sometimes, he would take on a partner for a while, but mostly acted on his own.

Mary Ann had two useful skills. She could find food and shelter in the bush and she had been educated in a girls' school. That meant she could go into town to find out what the police were doing, or get supplies. Nobody suspected this attractive, ladylike woman.

She was arrested a number of times, though, for small crimes, and once served three months before being released. After this, she stayed out of trouble for the sake of her children.

We don't know exactly what happened to Mary Ann. She probably died of pneumonia, after returning to her husband for a while. One night in 1869, Fred approached a woman called Mrs Bradford and asked her to look after a dying woman. Mrs Bradford took her in, but Mary Ann died that same night. The name the newspapers gave the dead woman was Louisa Mason, Mary Ann's fake name from Balmain.

Whatever did happen, she had lived the life she wanted to live, with the man she loved.

DID YOU KNOW...?

Australia's first architect was a convict. In 1814, Francis Greenaway was transported to Australia for fourteen years for forgery. He didn't have to work on any chain gangs, though. Governor Macquarie let him set up a business and he was pardoned in 1818, after he'd designed the Macquarie Lighthouse. Greenaway designed a lot of Sydney's most important buildings, which are still around today. Unfortunately, after Macquarie left in 1822, Greenaway was sacked from his job, due to government spending cutbacks. He refused to leave his government house, and lived there till he died in 1837.

ARTHUR ORTON
THE TICHBORNE CLAIMANT

In 1853, Roger Tichborne sailed off to South America after an argument with his rich, upper-class family over a girl he wanted to marry. A year later, he drowned in a shipwreck. That should have been the end of the story, but it wasn't.

Around the same time, another young man, a butcher's son, Arthur Orton, also sailed to South America. He didn't like working on a ship, so he ran away when the ship reached Chile. After eighteen months, he went home, but he didn't stay long. Like Roger, he had a fight with his family over a girl. He left for Australia.

Lady Tichborne, who lived in France, refused to believe that her darling boy was dead. Her husband thought she was crazy, but by 1866 both he and their younger son, Arthur Tichborne, had died. Now she could do what she wanted.

She put an advertisement in the papers, offering a large reward for anyone who could help her find Roger. The advert even reached Australia, where Arthur Orton had been living for thirteen years. He had settled in the New South Wales town of Wagga Wagga, where he worked as a butcher. He was broke and needed cash desperately.

Arthur wrote to Lady Tichborne, claiming he was Roger and asked could he have some money, please? As it happened, there were two former Tichborne servants living in Sydney, Andrew Bogle and Michael Guilfoyle. He would have to convince them first.

For some reason, both men agreed that he was Roger. Maybe he had offered them their old jobs back. Maybe he had promised to share the money. In any case, that was enough for Lady Tichborne. In December 1866, she paid for him to travel to France.

Here, the story becomes *really* weird. Arthur didn't look anything like Roger. Lady Tichborne's son had been slim and attractive. Arthur was fat and ugly and farted a lot.

He knew nothing about Roger's childhood, family or friends except what he had learned from Andrew and Michael.

Still, Lady Tichborne accepted him as her son. After all, the poor boy had been sick. He'd suffered a shipwreck. Naturally, he had forgotten.

She gave him an income of a thousand pounds a year. In those days, this was a fortune. If he'd been satisfied with it, he could have lived happily ever after and his story would never have made it into the history books.

But Lady Tichborne died. Arthur wasn't going to settle for a thousand pounds a year when he could have it all. Arthur knew he'd have to fight the family for it.

So started a very long trial, which cost everyone a lot of money and ended up costing Arthur much more. He managed to bribe some witnesses, including his own family. A man called Jean Luie said he was a sailor who had cared for Roger after the shipwreck. Unfortunately he turned out to be a con artist called Sorenson. In the end, Arthur's brother Charles admitted Arthur was his brother. Even Arthur's old girlfriend identified him.

In 1873, Arthur was sentenced to fourteen years for perjury (telling lies in court). When he came out in 1884, he admitted he'd lied.

Arthur Orton died in 1898, a lot poorer than he had hoped to be.

Could it happen today? Probably not the way it did. The world is a much smaller place, with aeroplanes and the Internet. And if Arthur did try to make a claim, a DNA test would settle the matter.

But we still love a good story. Even today, some people still believe Arthur was who he said he was.

So perhaps a modern Arthur Orton would get away with it for a while…

DID YOU KNOW…?

In the 1920s, Australian cat burglar George McCraig was working in New York and London. He was known as the Human Fly because he was so good at climbing buildings. When he wasn't stealing jewellery, George was working as a stuntman. Spiderman would have been jealous.

NED KELLY

Edward 'Ned' Kelly almost couldn't help getting into trouble with the law. His father, John 'Red' Kelly, was brought to Australia in chains from Ireland in 1841. His father's relatives, the Lloyds, were always getting into strife with the law. His mother Ellen's family, the Quinns, were another lawbreaking bunch. It would only have been surprising if he hadn't ever broken the law.

The Kellys were Irish and Catholic. To them, anyone English was an oppressor and Irish police were traitors. This is important, since in some ways, the Kelly gang formed because of an Irish policeman.

We're not certain exactly when Ned was born, but it was in about 1855. When his father died in 1866, his family moved to north-eastern Victoria. They had a farm, but it didn't earn them much and they probably stole to survive.

In his early teens, Ned worked with a bushranger called Harry Power. In 1870, the fifteen-year-old Ned was arrested for being Power's 'apprentice'. Charges were dropped because they couldn't be sure he was the right person, but later that year, he got six months in prison for assault and obscene language.

Ned and his brothers, Dan and James, often got into trouble, but Ned stopped for a while.

Remember that Irish policeman? His name was Fitzpatrick. He liked Ned's sister, Kate. The Kellys were never going to roll out the red carpet for him, but when he turned up to arrest Dan Kelly one day in 1878, he had a fight on his hands. Dan wasn't even there. Ellen, Kate and two others were. Fitzpatrick was lightly wounded. Fitzpatrick claimed that he had been attacked by Ned, Dan, Ellen, a neighbour called Williamson and a Kelly relative, William Skillion. Skillion, Williamson and Ellen were all arrested. Ellen was sentenced to three years in prison for attempted murder. Her judge was Redmond Barry, who ended up sentencing her son to death.

In October, policemen McIntyre, Kennedy, Scanlan and Lonigan went after Ned, Dan and their friends Joe Byrne and Steve Hart, who had gone into hiding. In the gun fight that followed, Lonigan was shot dead. Kennedy was wounded so badly that Ned finished him off – out of mercy, he later said. He covered him with a cloak and left.

They robbed banks in the small Victorian towns of Euroa and Jerilderie. In Jerilderie, they tied up the police and made the rest of the town's people go to the Royal Mail Hotel, where everyone enjoyed free drinks. There, Ned dictated what has become famous as the Jerilderie Letter. It was the length of a short book. He said he and his family and friends had been badly treated by sons of Irish bailiffs of English landlords.

Actually, the Kelly gang didn't do much bush-ranging. Their whole time as outlaws lasted about eighteen months. There was more murder, when Joe Byrne killed a former friend called Aaron Sherritt, whom he considered a traitor.

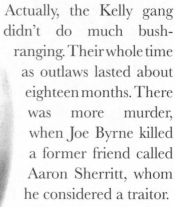

Now the police got serious. A special train was arranged to bring many policemen to Beechworth. Ned knew about this plan. He had plenty of supporters. Some were going to come and fight beside him against the police. The gang ripped up the tracks to derail the train outside the town of Glenrowan. Wearing new armour made from plough parts, they herded the people of Glenrowan into the local hotel – and waited. There was a party. Ned made the fatal mistake of letting the local schoolmaster, Thomas Curnow, take his family home.

Curnow went to warn the police to stop the train.

The police besieged the hotel. Ned had gone to warn his supporters. By the time he returned, Joe, Steve and Dan were dead. Their homemade armour hadn't helped much. Left alone, Ned now fought 34 police and received 28 wounds. Somehow, he survived to be tried for multiple murders in late October, 1880.

His trial was certainly unfair. Evidence that would have helped him was not used. Modern re-enactments, done according to modern law, have found him 'not guilty'.

But this was 1880. Redmond Barry condemned him to hang. First, he asked Ned if he had anything to say. Ned said that they would soon meet in a higher court.

On 11 November, he died with some dignity. His last words were 'Such is life'. He was twenty-five.

Interestingly, Redmond Barry died, quite suddenly, only two weeks after Ned.

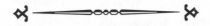

DID YOU KNOW...?

Ned Kelly's younger brother, James, was one of the few family members to go straight. After a few years of getting into trouble with the law in his teens, James settled down and became a much-respected, law-abiding citizen. He lived to a ripe old age, dying in 1946.

FRANCES KNORR
BABY FARMER

In the nineteenth century and even in the early twentieth, there was no pension for single mothers, as there is today. In those days, with no husband to support you, you were on your own. It was even worse if you gave birth to a child without being married. You would

have a hard time getting a husband or even a job, because this was considered shocking. So, many women who needed to work relied on baby farmers.

Baby farmers were people who acted as foster carers for poor women who were alone and needed to get jobs. You would take the baby to them and pay them to look after it while you worked, hoping you could see your child every now and then. The problem was, these people were out to make a profit. Looking after babies was not very profitable. You had to feed them and clothe them and that cost money. If you had too many children in your care, you wouldn't have room for more, and that meant less money. Besides, child care was hard work. Why bother to do that when you could kill them and keep taking money from their mothers, making excuses for why they weren't at home?

Frances Knorr was one such baby farmer and she ended up on the gallows.

Frances Thwaites arrived in Australia in 1887, after her affair with a soldier embarrassed her respectable English family. She worked in Sydney for a while before meeting and marrying Rudolph Knorr, a German waiter. The couple moved to Melbourne, then Adelaide, but in 1892, Rudi went to prison for selling furniture they didn't actually own yet.

Frances was on her own, with a baby daughter and no income. At this stage, perhaps she might have become the victim of a baby farmer herself, but she tried working as a dressmaker. That didn't work, so she stole enough money to get her and her child back to Melbourne. For a while, a man called Edward Thompson supported her, but he left her.

Desperate for money to live on, she took up baby farming. She didn't kill all the children she was caring for. Some were sold to families that didn't have children of their own. One went back to its mother. She moved house a lot, something that baby farmers often did, so that mothers wouldn't find out what had happened to their children. But when Rudi was released and the couple went back to Sydney, the bodies of three babies were found in the backyard of a house in Brunswick where she had lived. Frances, who was expecting her second child at the time, was arrested. After her baby's birth in 1893, she was put on trial for murder.

She wrote to Edward Thompson, asking him to support her with fake evidence, but the prosecution got hold of her letter to him and used it against her. Her husband begged for mercy for her, saying that she had an illness called epilepsy and didn't know what she was doing. It didn't help. Neither did a petition from the women of Victoria, who felt that men shouldn't be executing women for doing things that no man would ever have been forced to do. Despite these pleas, she was sentenced to death.

Just before she died at Pentridge Prison in early 1894, Frances Knorr found religion. She went to the gallows singing the hymn 'Abide With Me'. She even left a letter for the State Premier, advising how he could change the laws to prevent baby farmers from doing what she had done.

She was a sad case, but this would not have been of any comfort to the mothers of her victims.

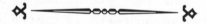

FREDERICK DEEMING

Pretty Kate Rounsefell had just arrived in Melbourne by train. She was looking forward to travelling on to Western Australia, where she was going to join her fiancé, Albert Williams. She had met him on the ship from Melbourne to Sydney and he had swept her off her feet.

As she stepped off the train, she was handed a telegram from her sister, Elizabeth. Police had told Elizabeth the truth about her fiancé. His name wasn't Albert Williams, or Baron Swanston as he had claimed to others, it was Frederick Deeming – and he was wanted for the murders of his wives and children. Even the engagement ring she was wearing had belonged to Emily, the wife he'd left hidden under the fireplace of their home in the Melbourne suburb of Windsor.

This was 1892. Elizabeth couldn't email Kate or ring her on a mobile phone. She could only hope that one of the four telegrams she sent would reach Kate. Luckily, one had.

The investigation began when the owner of a house in Windsor checked out a horrible smell from a bedroom. His tenant, a Mr Druin, had gone. The smell came from the rotting body of a woman whose throat had been cut and who had been shoved under the fireplace. Police found papers that belonged to a Mr Albert Williams and his wife Emily, who had arrived in Australia a year ago.

Clearly, Albert Williams was Mr Druin. Investigators also traced him to Western Australia, where he had gone under the name of Baron Swanston. He was living in a small town called Southern Cross. Deeming was arrested and brought back to Melbourne to stand trial.

Now, the whole horrible story came out. Frederick Deeming and his wife Marie had come from England in 1881, settling in the Sydney suburb of Balmain. They had two children, who went back with them to England when Deeming had to escape some debts. There, they had two more children. He'd been going by the name of Albert Williams at the time and another piece of paper found in Windsor told police where he had been living in England: Rainhill, a village near Liverpool.

The editor of the *Argus*, a Melbourne newspaper, decided this might make a good story. He contacted the newspaper's London journalist and asked him to go to Rainhill, to see what he could find out.

The journalist spoke to the mother of Emily Mather, who had gone to Australia with Albert Williams and never returned. Mrs Mather said there was a house he had rented in the area. He had never lived there, staying at a hotel instead. Perhaps there would be something interesting at the house.

Liverpool police were indeed very interested. They

found the bodies of Marie and her four children. Unfortunately, Deeming couldn't be tried for their murders in Australia, but he would be tried for Emily's murder.

Nobody can say he wasn't given a fair trial. He had a very good lawyer, a barrister called Alfred Deakin, who would one day be the Prime Minister of Australia. Deakin tried to prove that Deeming had been insane at the time of the murders. It didn't work, even though Deeming tried to prove his own insanity by telling the government doctor, Dr Shield, that his dead mother had told him to commit all those murders.

Just before his sentencing, he demanded that the court get on with it. He'd been kept waiting for four days, he complained, and he'd been in court since ten o'clock that morning. He wanted to be released, now! And he'd had about enough of that ugly bunch of jurors.

The jury obliged him. They did get on with their decision, finding him guilty of Emily's murder. On a cold morning in May, he gulped down his last glass of brandy and was hanged at the Old Melbourne Gaol, on the same gallows as Ned Kelly.

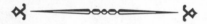

DID YOU KNOW...?

Most people who have heard of Redmond Barry only know him as the judge who sentenced Ned Kelly to death. In fact, he did a lot more than that for the city of Melbourne. He founded Melbourne University, the State Library and Museum of Victoria. Before there was a public library, he let people come to his house to read his own books. He gave much of his income to the poor. Even as a judge, he had a reputation for not being too hard on those he convicted - except, perhaps, for poor Ned Kelly.

JOHN AND SARAH MAKIN

ALL IN THE BABY-FARMING FAMILY

The Makins seemed like such a nice couple. They had four children of their own living with them, Florence, Clarice, Blanche and Daisy. When eighteen-year-old Amber Murray, unmarried mother of a little boy called Horace, first met them in 1892, she just knew the kindly couple would be the perfect foster parents for her child.

Amber had put an ad in the *Sydney Morning Herald*, asking for a kind, motherly person to adopt her little boy. She was willing to pay for this. She received a letter from a Mr and Mrs Makin in the Sydney suburb of Redfern, who said they had lost their own little boy and would be thrilled to take care of hers for ten shillings a week. They promised that her son would 'receive a mother's love and attention'.

When she arrived at their home, she found that they were baby farmers, looking after several other children. But the young mother hadn't heard about what some baby farmers got up to. And they must be all right, because they didn't have any problem with her wish to visit her child often. They even told her that they would be moving soon, to a place called Hurstville.

Somehow, the Makins managed to collect money from Amber weekly, while not letting her see her baby. They couldn't let her see him, of course. He was dead and buried in their garden. When they did move – as they had to, with all those little bodies buried in the backyard – it was to a suburb called Macdonaldtown, not to Hurstville.

They did take some babies with them, but of course, poor little Horace wasn't among them. John Makin took a baby for a visit to Amber's address. It had sores all over its face so perhaps she wouldn't have been suspicious even if she'd been at home. As it was, only her landlady was there and she had no idea what Horace looked like.

The Makin family left Macdonaldtown after only a few weeks. This was a mistake. When a man came in to install some pipes, he found the bodies of two dead babies. Police soon found five more. And that was only at the Macdonaldtown address. Altogether, the investigators ended up discovering twelve bodies.

The police tracked down the family to a nearby suburb called Chippendale. At this new home, there were no babies. The couple claimed that they had only ever looked after one child, whose parents had taken it back.

Police found several more bodies at the house in Redfern, including Amber Murray's little boy.

Now, the truth came out. The family was always on the move, going under different names. The Makins' daughters had known what was going on. The whole family was arrested, which must have been unusual for this kind of crime. The youngest child, Daisy, was only eleven years old.

Witness after witness spoke against John and Sarah Makin, including two of their own children. Clarice Makin said she had left home to work as a servant, but she remembered two babies staying with her parents in Macdonaldtown. She also recognised some clothing from the dead children.

Little Daisy broke down and cried, but agreed that her mother had brought two baby girls to the house in Macdonaldtown.

The evidence against them was very strong. It didn't take the jury long to find them guilty. John and Sarah Makin were condemned to death. Their daughters were allowed to go free.

On 15 August 1893, John Makin was hanged at Sydney Gaol. Sarah's life sentence was reduced and she ended up serving a fourteen-year sentence.

She was released in 1911.

SQUIZZY TAYLOR

Joseph Leslie 'Squizzy' Taylor was a thief, blackmailer, drug dealer and many other things, but he spent very little time in prison. His longest sentence was two years, but that was early in his career. Squizzy was very good at persuading witnesses and juries that they would be safer if they didn't upset him.

Squizzy Taylor was born in 1888 in the seaside town of Brighton, now a suburb of Melbourne. He got a job as an apprentice jockey, but soon found that crime paid much better.

Squizzy joined a gang called the Bourke Street Rats, where he learned his trade, starting with shoplifting and picking pockets. At first he was just fined or got short sentences for his crimes. When finally a judge sentenced him to two years for picking pockets in 1908, he told Squizzy that he was now a confirmed criminal, but Squizzy hadn't even started.

Squizzy Taylor didn't like taking risks when he could go for easy targets or get someone else to do the dangerous work. He began with blackmail. Blackmail was easy: you just had to threaten to report people who were doing something illegal and demand that they pay you not to tell the police.

Another crime that paid well was something known as 'the ginger game'. This was like the trick played, years later, by Jean Lee and her boyfriend. Squizzy would ask his girlfriend or another woman to take a man to a hotel room. Soon afterwards, one of his gang members would burst in pretending to be an angry husband and make the victim pay a large fee if he wanted to avoid a bashing or worse.

These schemes worked well, but weren't enough for Taylor. Robbery was even better. In 1913, he was almost certainly involved in killing Arthur Trotter, a salesman he and his friends were robbing, but there wasn't enough proof to convict him.

Three years later, an unlucky cab driver hired by Taylor and a gang member ended up dead because he realised that the equipment they were carrying was for a robbery. Taylor literally got away with murder when three witnesses who swore that they had seen the killing suddenly changed their minds. Squizzy was

sentenced on a much lesser charge and only spent a year in prison.

After World War I, the government made a big mistake. Pubs now had to close at 6.00 p.m. sharp. This provided a new source of income for crooks like Squizzy Taylor. 'Sly grog' shops sold drinks to people after hours. Squizzy supplied the shops with illegal alcohol and 'protected' them. 'Protection' meant that they had to pay him not to wreck their businesses. And if the business you were running was illegal anyway, you couldn't very well complain to the police.

Over the next few years, Squizzy robbed, 'protected', dealt in drugs, murdered and even, occasionally, acted as a police informer. This didn't make him very popular with other criminals.

Some of his gang members went to the gallows, but not Squizzy. He always managed to slide out of trouble. In the end, though, it wasn't the police who finished him off. It was another criminal.

In 1927, Daniel 'Snowy' Cutmore, who had been in Squizzy's gang before moving to Sydney, returned to Melbourne. Snowy was an enemy now. When he smashed up a business Squizzy was 'protecting', Squizzy was very angry. With two of his men, he went to Snowy's home in Fitzroy. Snowy was sick in bed, but he wasn't so sick he'd forgotten to protect himself. A gun lay hidden in the bed.

Squizzy and his two men broke into the room.

Squizzy shot Snowy. Snowy managed to snatch up his gun and shoot Squizzy before he died. Squizzy staggered from the room and climbed into the waiting taxi. One of his men went with him, but left him before the cab reached St Vincent's Hospital, where he died. He was buried in the Brighton Cemetery, where his grave can still be seen.

DID YOU KNOW...?

Most people leave money in clothes going into the washing machine. Lewis Moran, father of Melbourne's criminal Moran family, hid $14,000 in the oven. When someone turned it on, the notes shrank to the size of play-money. Luckily for him, a friend managed to arrange for a bank in Sydney to accept the cash.

THE SHARK ARM
KILLING

On Anzac Day in 1935, people enjoying the public holiday with a visit to Sydney's Coogee Aquarium got a rather special treat. A huge tiger shark on display suddenly vomited up a human arm.

The shark hadn't actually eaten the arm. It had swallowed a smaller shark, which had swallowed the arm. Then it had been captured for the aquarium.

There was a lot of excitement over the matter. The story and the photo of the arm were in all the newspapers. It came out that no shark had eaten the victim. The arm, which had a tattoo on it, had been cut off its body with a knife. Clearly, someone had committed murder. First, police had to find out whose arm this was.

This didn't take long. The tattoo helped. A man called Smith saw the photo in *Truth* newspaper and said the arm belonged to his brother James. James Smith had been a petty crook, so the police had his fingerprint on files and were able to confirm that it was his arm.

They visited James' wife, who told them that her husband had gone out fishing on 7 April and never returned. A forger friend of his, Patrick Brady, might be able to help them, she suggested. People in the area near Brady's home in Cronulla had seen the two men together. The real estate agent who rented Brady his house said that some stuff was missing from it. Heavy stuff. A big tin storage case (nearly big enough to hold a body, perhaps?), an anchor and some lead window weights had all disappeared.

When the detectives found Patrick Brady, he said that he'd seen Smith with two others, one of whom was a man called Reginald Holmes. Holmes was a boat builder. A boat which Smith had helped to build

had sunk. Holmes had lost money on it and was not happy with Smith. Not happy at all. They arrested Brady anyway, and then went to find Holmes.

When the detectives reached McMahon's Point, where Holmes lived, they found that Holmes had decided to kill himself in one of his own speedboats. As the boat sped through Sydney Harbour, he put a gun to his head to shoot himself, but messed up. He did manage to blow himself out of the boat, bleeding but relatively unharmed. Climbing back aboard, he tried to escape from the police, but after a thrilling two-hour chase, he finally stopped at a place called Watson's Bay and gave himself up. He said he hadn't realised it was the police chasing him. Nobody believed that. He was arrested.

As he was injured, Holmes was taken to hospital where the police put him under guard. A few days later, he told them that Patrick Brady had murdered James Smith and had threatened to kill him, or have one of his friends kill him, if he spoke to police about the murder.

Whether or not this was true, we may never know. Holmes was going to speak as a witness against Brady at an inquest, beginning on 12 June. The prosecution was relying on him.

Perhaps Brady really did threaten to have Holmes killed, because on the morning of 12 June, someone shot Holmes as he was driving his car under the Sydney Harbour Bridge. Two men were arrested for

Holmes' murder, but there wasn't enough evidence to convict them and they had to be released.

With no witness, now that Holmes was gone, no evidence and no body, the police had to release Brady.

The shark arm mystery has remained a mystery, even to this day.

DID YOU KNOW…?

In 1992, James Finch, who had served time for the 1973 Whiskey Au Go Go firebombing, made a truly weird request from his home in England. While he'd been in prison, someone had sliced off the top joint of his little finger. It was in a jar in the prison's museum. He wanted it back.

SNOWY ROWLES
THE PERFECT MURDER

What would be a crime novelist's worst nightmare? Many would say that what they fear most is that someone will use their books to help commit the perfect crime.

Arthur Upfield, a popular crime writer of the 1920s and 1930s, author of the 'Bony' mysteries, found out how this felt.

Upfield had had some novels published already in 1929, when he went to work as a boundary rider on Western Australia's Rabbit-Proof Fence.

He was working on a novel, *The Sands of Windee*, and wanted his fictional detective to try to solve a murder without a body. He hadn't come up with an idea yet for how this could be done and asked his workmates for suggestions. How, he asked one night at the campfire, could a murderer get rid of a body completely?

The answer came from a man called George Ritchie. George suggested that the body could be burned first. There would be bits of bone left over, but those could be sifted out from the ashes. The ashes could be scattered and the bones pounded down. What was left could be dissolved in acid.

It was a great idea, Upfield agreed. Perhaps it was *too* good. After all, the detective had to be able to solve the mystery in the end! He asked Ritchie to think about it and offered a pound as a reward for a flaw in the plan that would help the detective solve the crime.

Unfortunately, one of the other workers was a travelling stockman called Snowy Rowles. When Ritchie mentioned the problem to him one day, he started to think – and he wasn't thinking about a way to earn that pound, either!

Soon after, Upfield, Ritchie, Rowles and some others were discussing the problem again at Camel Station, where they all worked. Still no one had thought of a flaw. That was in October.

In December, James Ryan and George Lloyd, two men travelling with Rowles, disappeared. A prospector called Yates mentioned that he'd seen Rowles driving Ryan's car. Rowles had told him that the other two were walking through the scrub, but Yates hadn't seen them.

On Christmas Eve, Rowles, who still had the car, mentioned to Upfield that Ryan had decided to stay in Mount Magnet and had lent him the car. He told someone else that he'd bought the car.

In May 1930, a man called Louis Carron left his job at Wydgee Station with Rowles. No one ever saw him alive again, yet Rowles was seen cashing Louis' pay cheque. But Carron had friends who were worried for him, because he had been keeping in touch and nobody had heard from him in a while. Rowles had been seen in Carron's company. When Rowles didn't answer a question sent to him by telegram about Carron, the police were called.

By this time, everyone had heard of the 'perfect murder' from Upfield's new novel and the police found that not one, but three men had last been seen alive hanging out with Rowles. Detectives found some of Carron's belongings at a hut along the Rabbit-Proof Fence, including a wedding-ring which was definitely his. His wife had had it recut and the jeweller had accidentally soldered it with a lower grade of gold than the rest of the ring.

Rowles was arrested. It turned out that he was a burglar called John Thomas Smith, who had escaped from jail. That meant they could keep him in prison while checking out the evidence.

Upfield had to be a witness at the trial and meanwhile, the newspaper reports were published side by side with scenes from his book. No doubt it sold plenty more copies of the book for him!

Rowles was found guilty of the three murders and hanged in 1931.

As for Arthur Upfield, he not only had a great plot for that book, but he used the wedding-ring story in another book. No more giving ideas to murderers!

DID YOU KNOW...?

Better late than never... In 2008, 86 years after Colin Ross was executed at the Old Melbourne Gaol for the rape and murder of twelve-year-old Alma Tirtschke, he finally was pardoned by the Victorian government. Unfortunately, although he almost certainly didn't commit the crime, the sentence can't be overturned, because that would legally require a retrial and it's a little hard to retry a case like this after nearly a century.

THE PYJAMA GIRL

In September 1934, a farmer leading his prize bull home along a road near Albury found the body of a woman dressed in yellow silk pyjamas. Police had trouble identifying her. They couldn't even check dental records, because there was a bullet lodged in her jaw. Someone had shot her and then tried to burn her.

Because she couldn't be identified, the 'Pyjama Girl', as she became known, was taken first to Albury hospital to be put on ice, then to Sydney University, where she was put into a tank of a preserving liquid called formalin.

After a few months, police interviewed an Italian waiter, Tony Agostini, who had lived in Sydney before moving to Melbourne. His wife, Linda, had disappeared around the time the Pyjama Girl turned up. He looked at the photo of the dead woman and denied it was his wife. He said that Linda had left him about a year ago and he had no idea where she was.

At that point, the police didn't take it any further.

For ten years, the Pyjama Girl lay in her formalin bath at the university. Then the New South Wales Police Commissioner, William Mackay, re-opened the case. He arranged for the Pyjama Girl to be removed from the tank. Make-up artists and hairdressers made her look presentable and, hopefully, like she had during her life. Sixteen people who had known Linda Agostini were asked to take a look at the body. Seven of them said they recognised her.

Mackay knew Tony Agostini personally. He was a waiter at Mackay's favourite Sydney restaurant, Romano's, where he had been working since moving from Melbourne.

He rang the restaurant and asked to speak to Agostini. He told him what had happened.

Tony broke down and confessed. He said that Linda had made his life miserable. She had a very bad temper and got especially violent after she had been drinking. She drank often. One night, he said, he had woken to find her standing over him with a gun. He had wrestled with her for the gun, to stop

her shooting him. The gun had gone off by accident while they fought and she had been killed.

Agostini said that he panicked. Instead of contacting the police, he had put her body in his car and driven through the night, along the Hume Highway towards Albury. He had thrown the body into a ditch, poured petrol on it and tried to burn it. It had begun to rain, so the body didn't burn completely. Agostini said he'd returned to his car and driven back to Melbourne.

When he was put on trial, the jury didn't take long to reach a decision. He wasn't convicted of murder, but of the lesser crime of manslaughter, because the death wasn't intended. He was sentenced to six years of hard labour, but he served only four before he was deported to Italy, where he lived the rest of his life.

There are some strange bits to this story. Tony and Linda were living in Melbourne when this killing was supposed to have happened. Albury is on the border of New South Wales and Victoria, hundreds of kilometres away from their home. Why drive all that way to dump a body?

When asked what he wanted done with the body, after conviction, Agostini said he didn't care, because it wasn't his wife.

A Sydney woman called Jeanette Rutledge had been saying that the dead woman was her daughter, Anna Philomena Morgan, but she had mental problems and police didn't believe her.

Was it Anna Philomena Morgan? If so, what *did* happen to Linda Agostini? If her husband hadn't killed her, why did he say he had? And then why did he change his story? Right until he left for Italy, he denied having killed the Pyjama Girl. He was in trouble with an Italian criminal organisation, the Camorra. Perhaps he felt safer in jail than out!

These days, it might be possible to do a DNA test on any living relatives Linda might have, to see if the body was hers. Otherwise, we may never know.

DID YOU KNOW...?

Archaeologists digging at Melbourne's former prison, Pentridge, found some bones that probably belong to the bushranger Ned Kelly. The skull was missing, as it was stolen in 1978.

CAROLINE GRILLS

Caroline Grills was exactly the sort of person you would have wanted for a grandmother. She was a tiny thing, only about 1.22 metres in height, with a kind, smiling face. She had been happily married for many years and had children, grandchildren and many friends. When visiting, she always brought delicious food – homemade, of course.

What you *really* wouldn't want to do was have afternoon tea with her.

In the 1940s and early 1950s, rat poison contained a nasty ingredient called thallium. If you swallowed it, you got horrible stomach pains, your hair fell out and you went blind. Finally, you would die. In most Australian states, anyone buying poison had to sign a special book, but in New South Wales anyone could buy rat poison without signing anything. Best of all, it was easy to put in food or drink and had no smell or taste. The perfect way to kill an unwanted family member!

But Caroline had other ideas. Her first victim was her stepmother, Christina Mickelson. When Caroline's father, Mr Mickelson died, he had left his house to Christina for her lifetime, then to Caroline.

Whilst Christina lived in the lovely Sydney suburb of Ryde, Caroline and her husband lived in the not-so-nice suburb of Gladesville, where there were a lot of – yuk! – rats. Christina was 87 and Caroline thought – how long could she live anyway? Why not speed things up just a little? Poor Christina died in agony and Caroline got the house.

After this success, Caroline decided that it might be good to have a second house. Her husband Richard was going to inherit one in the Blue Mountains, from a relative, Mrs Angelina Thomas. The old lady was, after all, 84 years old. Why couldn't she just die?

Early in 1948, Caroline's homemade cakes and pikelets made sure she did.

Caroline had something to gain by her first two

murders. But now, she started killing for fun. It made her feel good to see her victims sick and dying while she had this wonderful secret that only she knew.

Her next victim was her husband's brother-in-law. John Lundberg was a strong, healthy man. Nobody would have expected him to become sick. But after a holiday spent with Richard and Caroline, he did – losing his hair, going blind and finally dying in October 1948. Just to be fair to her own side of the family, Caroline also finished off her brother's widow, Mary Anne Mickelson.

After this, Caroline's luck started to run out. John Lundberg's widow, Eveline, became very sick, suffering cramps and going bald and blind. Of course, the kindly Caroline visited her with food and made her tea. Eveline's daughter, Christine Downey, and her husband, John, who played cards with Caroline, also became ill. After hearing in the news of a poisoning murder, they began to wonder. Their symptoms sounded familiar. Could sweet Aunt Carrie be poisoning them? .

The Downeys spoke to the police, who said they needed proof and suggested that they get some samples of Caroline's food. John Downey managed to save some poisoned tea and they had their proof.

Caroline was arrested, to the horror of her loving husband. He couldn't believe his wife would do anything so dreadful.

She sat smiling through her trial and joking with

the police. In October 1953, she was found guilty and sentenced to life imprisonment in Long Bay jail.

Caroline lived till 1960, charming everyone in the prison. The other prisoners affectionately called her Aunt Thally. Even the staff liked her. They probably didn't try her homemade cakes, though.

DID YOU KNOW...?

'Pretty' Dulcie Markham was a gangster's moll in the 1930s. She just adored men with guns. And they adored her too, with her film-star looks. The trouble with gunmen was that they didn't last long. Other men with guns or knives killed them. Some of her eight boyfriends killed each other over her. Dulcie must have decided she'd had enough, because finally she married a nice man who wasn't a criminal. She might have lived happily ever after, but died in a fire in 1973 when she fell asleep smoking.

JEAN LEE
LAST WOMAN TO BE HANGED
IN AUSTRALIA

When Jean Lee was born in Sydney in 1919, no one would have thought she would end up on the gallows. Her family lived in North Sydney, the nicer part of the town. She did well at her studies and was good at sport. Everyone liked her.

Suddenly, at the age of only fourteen, she dropped out of school. At nineteen she married. The marriage didn't last and by the time she was 23, she'd thrown over her old life, leaving her child with her mother and going to Brisbane.

During World War II, Jean, who liked to party, found plenty of soldiers to have fun with. She had also discovered the world of crime. In 1949, she and her boyfriend, Bobby Clayton, went back to Sydney, where they made good use of Jean's beauty. Another friend, Norman Andrews, joined them.

What they would do was this: Jean would choose some lonely-looking man and take him into the back seat of a car. After a short time, Bobby would interrupt them, pretending to be her angry husband and threatening to bash the man up if he wasn't given money. This worked nicely, but towards the end of the year, the three crooks decided to head for Melbourne, where they could find new victims.

While having a drink at the University Hotel in Carlton, they met an old man, Bill Kent. Bill was happy to chat with them. He was a bookie and the Melbourne Cup had just been run. He would certainly have plenty of money from bets. Their plan was to get him alone for a while so they could find out where the money was and steal it.

Jean suggested they all go back to Bill's home, a boarding house. Bill agreed and they walked to the house in Dorritt Street. Jean was very good at persuading men to do what she wanted and Bill certainly enjoyed her company, but when she couldn't get the money off him, things began to get nasty.

The three criminals tied Bill to a chair. They hit him with a piece of wood, smashed a beer bottle on his head and demanded to know where the money was.

Around nine o'clock, they left the room. One of them said, 'Goodnight, Bill, I'll see you tomorrow.' But Mrs Hayward, who lived in the next room, was suspicious. First there had been a lot of noise, which she thought was a party. Now, suddenly, it was very quiet. Too quiet.

She called the police who arrived to find Bill, dead. Someone had strangled him with one hand. They arrested Jean, Bobby and Norman at the Great Southern Hotel in Spencer Street, in the early hours of the morning. The trio had been partying at a nightclub. They were planning to leave the state; Jean had plane tickets for Adelaide.

Bobby insisted that he had left the room early and Norman and Jean had done it all. At first, Jean refused to say anything. Then she admitted she had hit the old man and claimed that no one else was involved. She couldn't possibly have strangled Bill, though; that would have taken someone much stronger. She was clearly protecting her boyfriend, but that didn't help her when she was tried for murder.

The trial lasted only five days. On 25 March 1950, the court found them all guilty and sentenced them to hang. Jean appealed against the sentence, but failed. People didn't like to see a woman hanged, but whether or not Jean had actually killed the old man, she had been involved in his torture. And she didn't even seem to be sorry.

In the end, she probably didn't know what was being done to her. The night before she was due to hang, 19 February 1951, Jean screamed and cried and protested that she was innocent. She was sedated and carried to the gallows in a chair.

She was the last woman in Australia to be executed.

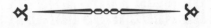

DID YOU KNOW...?

The Melbourne branch of the Painters and Dockers Union, which had a lot of criminal members, ran a strange election in 1971. Anyone else would have simply counted the votes and elected whoever got the most. But the two men standing for the top job both wanted it very badly. To make sure he won, Billy Longley sent his men to machine-gun the ballot boxes at Williamstown, his competition's car and the union offices in Port Melbourne. Then he found out that Pat Shannon, the other candidate, had sent his men even earlier to 'stuff' the ballot boxes with his own votes, while the voters waited at gunpoint. A very interesting idea of democracy!

ERIC COOKE
THE NEDLANDS MONSTER

If you had lived in the city of Perth in the late 1950s and early 1960s, you would have felt quite safe. It was a small town. People didn't bother to lock their doors. Nothing could possibly happen to you in such a peaceful place, you would have thought.

You would have been wrong.

Nobody really knows why Eric Cooke started killing people. Later, he said that he just wanted to hurt someone.

Was it because of his looks or his violent childhood? He was born with a deformed face – a cleft lip – which made him ugly. Other children bullied him at school. His father bashed him when he tried to protect his mother from his dad's violent outbursts.

Was it because he kept having accidents

at work, which might have damaged his brain, perhaps? We don't know.

Whatever his problems, he was married, with seven children. Nobody would have dreamed this good husband and father was spending his nights killing people. Certainly not his wife.

Before he became a murderer, Eric Cooke had already spent time in jail, for burglary and starting fires. He had actually burned down a church because he was annoyed at not making it into the choir. He had burned down a theatre just because he felt like it.

In 1959, a woman called Jillian Brewer was murdered in her bed. She had been stabbed and hacked about the face. She hadn't been robbed or raped. Someone, it seemed, just liked killing. This might have been one of Cooke's first murders.

But Eric didn't just stab his victims. Late one night in April 1961, a couple in a parked car saw a man about to shoot them. They managed to duck just in time to avoid being killed, though they both suffered wounds.

Perhaps Eric was annoyed that he had failed to kill that time. Only an hour later, a man called George Walmsley opened his door to a knock and was shot in the head.

Police coming to George's house made such a noise that they woke up a neighbour. She went to chat about it with her lodger, a young student called

John Sturkey. Poor John was dying from a bullet in his head.

In the morning, yet another shooting was reported. Luckily that victim, an accountant, had an operation and survived.

The last murder happened in August that year. A girl called Shirley McLeod was shot while she was babysitting.

But this was the beginning of the end for Eric. He made the mistake of leaving his .22 rifle hidden by the Canning River, where an elderly couple found it only a week later. Police took it away as evidence, replacing it with another gun of the same kind. Then they waited for him to come back to collect it. Two weeks later, he did, and they arrested him. He didn't fight. He even showed them where he had hidden another gun.

At his trial, Cooke bragged about his career as a criminal, taking credit for several hundred crimes of different kinds, including theft and knocking people over with his car. He actually admitted to two murders of which he hadn't been accused – the murder of Jillian Brewer and of a teenager called Rosemary Anderson, whom he had knocked over in his car. The judge didn't believe him about those, because two other men, Douglas Beamish and John Button, were serving time for them. It wasn't until years later that evidence showed he'd been telling the truth.

Either way, it wouldn't have made any difference to Cooke, who was executed at Fremantle Prison in October 1964. He was the last person to hang in Western Australia.

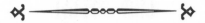

DID YOU KNOW...?

In 1970, thief Joey Turner, who had stolen thousands of dollars from security company MSS, was arrested because he'd forgotten to take some of the stolen money out of his pockets when his wife washed his clothes. Joey tried to iron out the wet $2 notes, but hadn't the patience to wait till they were dry. He spent some money at the souvenir shop of the Southern Cross Hotel in Melbourne. When the shop assistant took the still-damp money to the bank, the clerk got suspicious and checked out the serial numbers, just in case.

MURRAY BERESFORD ROBERTS
CON ARTIST

He was born in New Zealand in 1919 and his name was Murray Roberts … or was it John Cook? John Jackson? How about Sir Leonard Jackson? Lord Russell?

This man used a lot of names during his life of deceit. The name he was born with though, was Murray Beresford Roberts and he spent his first 27 years in New Zealand. He began to study medicine at the University of Otago, but never bothered to finish his degree.

That didn't stop him from practising medicine. In 1941 he worked as a locum, a doctor who covers for another doctor who is busy, sick or on holidays. He was caught out by the authorities and fined 50 pounds.

That didn't put Murray off; next, he posed as a high-ranking army doctor.

Perhaps he decided that he'd fooled all the people he could in New Zealand. Whatever the reason, he moved to Australia after the war in 1946.

Murray managed to get several jobs by claiming to have a lot of university degrees he didn't have.

In Western Australia, in 1949, he married his first wife, a typist called Dorothy. For some reason, he used a fake name, John Malcolm Cook. The marriage lasted six years, with one son. It would be interesting to know what he told his wife about how he was earning a living.

Murray just couldn't help himself. He liked playing doctors and teachers (he didn't have teaching qualifications, any more than he had medical ones). He was good-looking and spoke beautifully. Everyone believed him. Even some people who had worked with him still liked him after they found out the truth.

In Melbourne, during 1954, he made money under the name of 'Professor Sir Leonard Jackson', saying he was a prosecutor in the Petrov royal commission, which was checking out spying in Australia. When he needed to speak to a prisoner in Goulburn jail, in New South Wales, he pretended to be a surgeon. He even offered to do a muscle graft at the Goulburn Base Hospital the next day.

Luckily for the poor patient, he never turned up!

In Tasmania, in 1956, he took 50 pounds from a truck driver as a deposit on a house. The trouble was, he didn't actually own the house he was selling.

His next scam was in Sydney, where he posed as

the new Governor-General of Australia! It worked long enough to get him a luxury hotel suite, but not long enough. After doing prison time, he was shipped back to Tasmania to stand trial for the cons he'd carried out there.

Unfortunately, Murray still couldn't see that he'd done anything wrong – and he couldn't resist playing more roles. In Brisbane, in 1958, he claimed to be a judge of the New Zealand Supreme Court. He left for Sydney without paying his hotel bill and was charged with theft.

Still, he hung around in Sydney, where he posed as a Baron Alfred von Krupp and promised Manly a brand new car park. The Sydney public was amused, but the court wasn't; he got another jail sentence.

By this time, he'd been divorced from Dorothy for five years, and married again, to a woman called Beryl. Poor Beryl didn't know her husband was called Murray Roberts. She thought he was John Jackson. Again, the court was not amused. In March, he got another prison term, for lying to the marriage registrar, and soon after, a divorce.

Later in his life, his scams became nastier. In 1962, he played the role of a doctor again – Lord Porter, doctor to the royal family – and this time, he got 400 pounds out of his victim as payment for a cancer operation. He managed to get as far as Darwin before he was caught and brought back. This time, the jail sentence was four years.

Naughty Murray hadn't been out of jail for long when he proposed marriage to a woman called Joyce and sweet-talked 4000 pounds out of her. Luckily for Joyce, he was caught before he could get far.

After turning to drink, he died in 1974, choking on his own vomit in a New Zealand hotel room.

Was Murray Roberts a success as a con artist? In some ways, yes, for he did fool a lot of people. But then, he also kept being caught!

DID YOU KNOW...?

Double trouble...? Most identical twins have fun confusing their teachers, parents and friends. Identical twin robbers, Peter and Doug Moran (known as the After Dark Bandits) worked together to fool police and witnesses in the late 1970s. They dressed alike and gave each other alibis. It worked for two years, but in 1979, they were caught after Peter almost killed a policeman at a bank in Heathcote, Victoria. Both got long jail sentences.

RONALD RYAN
LAST PERSON TO HANG IN AUSTRALIA

Ronald Ryan was a small-time crook whose death made him a lot more famous than his life ever had. People are still arguing over whether he actually did murder a prison guard, the crime for which he was executed. Still, his death changed Australia forever.

Ronald was born in Melbourne in 1925, to a poor family. His mother couldn't look after him properly, so he and his sisters were taken away and put into homes for neglected children. Ronald did well at the boys' home where he was living, but he ran away when he was fourteen. For several years, he worked honestly to support his mother and sisters, but then he began to commit crimes. Several times he went to jail for robberies and forgery, but each time he came out, he fell back into crime.

In December 1964, he was in jail again at Pentridge Prison, serving fourteen years for armed robbery. For his wife, this was the last straw. She was going to divorce him. Now, Ronald made the decision that would end up costing his life and the life of a prison guard. To save his marriage, he would escape from Pentridge. He would take his wife and three children to Brazil, where they would be safe from the Australian law.

Ronald arranged his escape with another prisoner, Peter Walker. After overcoming a guard, Helmut Lange, and stealing his rifle, the two men ran for it, alarms sounding loudly. Then the tragedy happened. Another guard, George Hodson, was running just behind Peter Walker. At this point, we're not sure exactly what happened. Ryan might have shot Hodson to protect Walker. Later, a guard said he had fired a shot from a tower, but changed his story. Anyway, whatever really happened, Hodson died.

Ryan and Walker were on the run for nearly three weeks. While they were hiding in Melbourne, Walker shot and killed someone who recognised them. Finally, they escaped to Sydney, where they were hoping to get help from a criminal called Lennie McPherson. McPherson promised to arrange their escape to Brazil, but then he turned them in to the police instead.

Back in Melbourne, Peter Walker was sentenced to twelve years for the manslaughter of the man he had shot before they went to Sydney.

Ryan was now on trial for the murder of George Hodson. There was a lot of argument over whether or not it would have been possible for him to shoot Hodson, but the jury found him guilty. Justice Starke, a judge who was against the death penalty, was forced to condemn Ryan to hang. Starke never forgave himself.

Now the fuss began. Appeals were made and rejected. There were protests and petitions. Barry Jones, who would later become a federal Minister for Science, led a committee against Ryan's execution. Three newspapers which usually supported the government campaigned for mercy.

Even some members of the jury begged the State Premier, Henry Bolte, to use his power to stop the death sentence. Most of the jury had wanted to find Ryan not guilty, but had been persuaded to change their minds. After all, nobody had been executed in Australia since 1951. Since then, death sentences had always been changed to life imprisonment. They had really believed that this would happen now.

But Henry Bolte wanted this execution to go ahead. A few years before, he had been stopped from executing another criminal. This time, he would show who was boss! Perhaps he believed that being firm on this matter would get him more votes in the next election.

In February 1967, Ronald Ryan went to the gallows. Some of the journalists who had to watch the hanging threw up in the toilets.

Outside the prison, 3000 protesters gathered and at the exact time he was executed, many people around Australia observed a three-minute silence.

That was the end of capital punishment in

Australia. It was now clear that death sentences weren't popular any more. One by one the states changed their laws. In 1985, Australia scrapped it altogether. During that time, nobody else was actually executed.

For sure, Ronald Ryan would have preferred capital punishment to end in a better way, but still, this petty crook made a very big difference.

DID YOU KNOW...?

It's possible to go from national hero to national villain. Millionaire businessman Alan Bond has been both. In 1978, he was named Australian of the Year. After he won the America's Cup yacht race in 1983, he was a national hero. A TV mini-series was made about his victory. By 1997, his business empire was crumbling and he had been declared bankrupt. He had taken a large sum of money from a company called Bell Resources, which he controlled, to prop up his own company, the Bond Corporation. Many people lost their money because of this. It got him a seven-year jail term, but he served only four, and his family paid back only a tiny amount of the $1.8 billion he owed. In 2008, Bond was back on the 'Rich 200 List', almost as rich as he was before.

DEREK ERNEST PERCY
CHILD KILLER

Derek Percy has been in jail since July 1969, Victoria's longest-serving prisoner. When he went to prison, the Apollo 11 astronauts had just walked on the moon. Television in Australia was black and white. You could buy four lollies for a cent. Computers filled whole rooms and had about the power of your pocket calculator. There was no Internet.

He was in jail for the torture and murder of twelve-year-old Yvonne Tuohy on 20 July 1969. Police suspect that he committed several other child murders, because he was near all those places at the time.

The trouble is, he can't be DNA tested because, strictly speaking, he hasn't been convicted. He was found not guilty due to insanity and put in jail 'at the Governor's pleasure'. That meant that every now and then his case would be reviewed and if it was felt that he was no longer a danger, he might be released.

So far, he hasn't been.

Derek Percy's family moved around a lot during his childhood. He had to keep changing schools. Because of that, he never had much chance to make friends and didn't really try.

His diary was his only friend. One day his parents happened to look at it and were horrified by what they read. He had fantasies about torturing and killing children. The local doctor told them it was just a stage he was going through. Nothing was done.

Derek joined the navy when he was nineteen and did well. He was even considered for officer training. But he was still keeping that diary.

On Sunday, 20 July, Yvonne Tuohy, who lived in the Victorian coastal town of Warneet, suggested to her friend Shane Stiller that they go for a walk on the beach. They had sandwiches and Shane took along a small axe to chop wood for a billy tea.

On the beach, they stopped for a moment, deciding in which direction to go. Shane saw a man watching them from a car nearby. They had walked in different direc- tions and were turning back when the man grabbed Yvonne. He de- manded that Shane come to him as well, but Shane held up his axe, defending himself. He turned and ran for help. Unfortunately, the picnicking family Shane found thought he was just playing. By then, it was too late. Percy had driven off with Yvonne.

He did help police by describing the man and the car. He described a sticker on the car, which was a navy insignia.

Yvonne's body was soon found, tied and gagged.

The homicide squad went to the Cerberus Navy Base nearby. They found Percy washing the blood from his clothes. They found the diary in his locker. Shane identified his car in the car park. Later, he identified Percy at a line-up. They had enough evidence to arrest him.

After the trial, at which Shane spoke as a witness, he never really recovered. In those days, nobody had thought of counselling. Poor Shane was told to get over it and get on with his life. He never did. He drank and suffered from depression. In 2005, he disappeared.

While Percy had certainly committed this murder, the question was what to do with him. In those days, the death sentence was still a part of law, but no one had been executed in Australia since Ronald Ryan in 1967. If he were given a life sentence, he would be out in twenty years, free to commit more murders.

Nobody sane, it was decided, could possibly have done what Percy had done. Declaring him insane and making his sentence 'at the Governor's pleasure' was the only way to keep him behind bars indefinitely.

In jail, he collected stamps and played carpet bowls. When personal computers arrived, he bought one and learned how to program it. He got a pension from the navy and saved $30,000.

And he kept materials in his cell that told police he hadn't felt at all sorry for what he had done. Psychiatrists checked him over the years. They offered him the chance to join groups for therapy. He wasn't interested.

In the end, they concluded that Derek Percy had no mental condition they could treat. He wasn't insane – just evil.

His case was reviewed in 1998, along with a number of other killers who were being held at the Governor's pleasure. He was the only one still considered too dangerous to release.

In 2005, police interviewed him about a number of other murders committed in the 1960s, but he simply said he didn't remember. They couldn't take his DNA to check, because they only have the right to do that for convicted prisoners and he isn't convicted. If he had been convicted, he would have to be released at some stage. The murders may remain mysteries forever.

And Percy will probably die in jail.

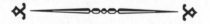

DID YOU KNOW...?

In 2005, two Australians who'd robbed a bank in the US state of Colorado were caught the very next day. Anthony Prince and Luke Carroll grinned at the cameras, waving their stolen money around. They wore masks for the robbery, but didn't bother to take off the badges they usually wore in the nearby ski shop where they worked. Their Australian accents also gave them away. Instead of a getaway car, they used their work passes to catch a handy ski lift. Australian newspapers called them 'Dumb and Dumber'.

JOHN STUART AND JAMES FINCH
FIREBOMBERS

When John Stuart, a Brisbane criminal, decided to firebomb the Whiskey Au Go Go nightclub in 1973, he sent all the way to England for help. James Finch had been in prison with him, serving a fourteen-year sentence before being deported back to Britain.

The Whiskey Au Go Go was one of forty nightclubs in Brisbane in the 1970s. Nightclubs were easy places to threaten in those days. They were crowded. It would be hard to get out if there was an emergency.

Due to poor planning, the windows were sealed, replaced with air conditioners. Some of the exit doors were locked. The carpets had rubber underlay, so that when they burned, they would release poisonous carbon monoxide gas.

Extortion gangs in Brisbane threatened to firebomb nightclubs if they weren't paid regular 'protection' money. The Whiskey Au Go Go management refused. Firebombing this place would be a warning to the others. The gang standing over the Whiskey paid Stuart to organise an attack.

Stuart made his plans carefully. Finch and a man

called Hamilton would do the job. They had black balaclavas and petrol drums. There was another man to drive the getaway car.

As a criminal known to police, Stuart might be suspected, so he took care to cover his tracks. He contacted Brian Bolton, a journalist he knew. Two Sydney men, he said, were planning to firebomb a nightclub, he wasn't sure when or where. He suggested that Bolton should go around the nightclubs with him and warn the owners.

On 7 March, 100 people enjoyed live music played by two bands, the Delltones and Trinity. At 2 a.m., Finch and Hamilton leapt from their stolen car. Finch held two petrol drums and Hamilton took off the cap. They threw the drums inside the door, where the petrol spilled on to the floor, and threw in a match.

With a whoosh, the fire began. It roared up the stairs and the air conditioning system spread poisonous carbon monoxide fumes through the air.

People screamed and scrambled over each other to get out. Some managed to break the windows and leap out on to the footpath, five metres below. But fifteen people died, ten men and five women.

Stuart left a note for Bolton at his newspaper, saying he'd been waiting for him from 8.55 till 10.40 p.m. – where had Bolton been?

Despite all the covering of tracks, police arrested Stuart and Finch on 12 March, less than a week after the firebombing. Hamilton was missing, probably dead.

To get the charges going quickly, police charged Finch and Stuart with one murder, of a woman called Jennifer Davie.

Stuart and Finch pleaded not guilty. They swallowed wire crosses, as a protest. Being in hospital didn't stop them being tried and convicted.

They appealed. They complained that they had been unfairly treated, that there had been too much publicity, making it impossible to get a fair trial. In November 1977, Stuart climbed on to the roof of his jail and used bricks and guttering to write a message: 'Innocent – victim of police verbal'. He even wrote poetry. None of it helped.

In 1979, a heart infection killed him in his cell.

Finch spent his time in prison protesting his

innocence. He wrote letters. Journalists supported him. There were even groups who were trying to get him released. There were claims that the confessions had been made up by police and weren't genuine. For years after the event, the men's guilt was questioned.

One of Finch's supporters, Cheryl Cole, actually married him.

Eventually, he was released and deported to Britain, leaving his wife behind. She did travel to England for a few months, but he treated her badly. She returned home.

Thinking he was safe, Finch admitted to a journalist that he and the others charged were guilty of the firebombing after all. When the Queensland government pointed out that he'd only been convicted of one murder and could be brought back to stand trial for the others, he backtracked, saying he'd been confused.

Whoops!

DID YOU KNOW...?

The 1970s were a good time for shoplifters in England. In fact, a group of Australian criminals, the Kangaroo Gang, travelled to the UK especially to shoplift. They worked in teams, usually sending in one member to cause trouble while the rest of them helped themselves to the goods. This wasn't a case of pinching a bag of sweets from a supermarket or a pair of jeans from a clothes shop either. One team actually stole a chimpanzee from the Harrods Zoo in London!

ROBERT TRIMBOLE

On 15 July 1977, furniture store owner Donald Mackay disappeared from the car park of a pub in the New South Wales town of Griffith. He was never seen again. At midnight, police found his blood-spattered white van and some spent cartridges in the car park.

Donald wasn't just a shopkeeper. He had worked hard to try to stop people in the area from growing and selling the drug marijuana. The first time he told police about it, the farmers just paid small fines. Then, in 1975, Donald found out about a much bigger crop being grown at a nearby place called Coleambally. Most of the growers and sellers went to jail. Donald had succeeded, but this incident ended up killing him. Defence lawyers saw a list of people who had reported their clients to the police. Now they knew their enemy.

Robert Trimbole also lived in Griffith. At first, he worked honestly as a panel beater, then with another man, fixing pinball machines. In 1972, he bought a restaurant, the Texas Tavern.

But by 1975, he didn't need the Texas Tavern any more and sold it. Robert was rich from selling marijuana. He owned many properties.

The men who had been fined during the first drug raid were related by marriage to his business partner,

Giuseppe Sergi. Giuseppe's brother-in-law, Francesco Sergi, was one of the men caught in the big raid.

Donald Mackay had to go.

Robert Trimbole went to Melbourne, where he had a chat with another business partner, Gianfranco Tizzoni. Tizzoni knew someone who could organise a hit man.

The hit man, Jim Bazley, agreed to do the job for $10,000. He rang Donald from the town of Jerilderie, 160 kilometres from Griffith, saying he wanted to buy a houseful of furniture. Donald was busy that day. He sent a salesman, Harold Pursehouse, to meet him at the Flag Inn, Jerilderie. After waiting in his car for two hours, Harold left, but said later that he'd seen a man watching him.

Three days later, Donald disappeared. Robert made sure he had an alibi. He was in a Sydney restaurant at the time.

Donald was dead, though nobody could find his body, but the marijuana industry in the area was finished. Trimbole and the other marijuana dealers started to sell heroin instead. It paid better anyway.

In 1979, a drug boss called Terry Clark asked Robert to arrange for the deaths of two drug couriers, Douglas and Isabel Wilson, who had been talking to the police. Again, Jim Bazley got the job and killed the couple, but he messed it up. Their bodies were found only a month later. He hadn't parked their car at Melbourne Airport as he was supposed to, and Tizzoni and Trimbole did this instead. Trimbole told Tizzoni to get rid of their car keys and speeding ticket. Tizzoni threw them into a stormwater drain.

Police caught Bazley in Sydney when he was driving a stolen car. He received a nine-year sentence for armed robbery, which ended up as a life sentence. Tizzoni was caught with a car boot full of marijuana. Terrified, he told police a lot of things they needed to know. He showed them the stormwater drain, where the keys had fallen on a ledge.

Robert Trimbole escaped from Australia in 1981, on a false passport. In London, he was arranging weapons for the IRA, an Irish terrorist organisation. He went to Ireland under the name of Michael Hanbury. There, in 1985, the Irish police arrested him for a small crime. Unfortunately, Australia and Ireland didn't have any arrangements by which he could have been sent home to face trial. He had to be released.

Robert wasn't taking any chances. He left Ireland for Spain that night. But while he never went to jail for his crimes, he didn't live much longer. In 1987, he died of a heart attack.

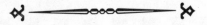

DID YOU KNOW...?

Just before Christmas 1967, Prime Minister Harold Holt went for a swim at Victoria's Cheviot Beach and disappeared, never to be seen again. Most people believe that he simply drowned. He was a strong swimmer, but he wasn't young, he had a bad shoulder and the sea was very rough. None of these facts have prevented conspiracy theories from springing up. One theory is that the CIA murdered him because he was planning to take Australia's troops out of Vietnam. Another theory says he was a Chinese spy and that a submarine took him to China. There was even a story that he ran off to France with a girl-friend and had been sneaking in and out of Australia till his death in the 1980s. A swimming pool in Melbourne has been named after him.

JAMES MILLER
THE KILLER WHO DIDN'T —
THE TRURO MURDERS

James Miller is in South Australia's Yatala Prison, for the murders of six women he didn't actually kill. The man who did kill them died long ago.

James was like a weak boy who hangs out with a bully, watching him bash people up and then complains, 'I wasn't doing nothing!' when the teacher punishes him.

In the early 1970s, James Miller, a small-time crook, was in prison. One of his fellow prisoners was a cheerful, good-looking boy called Chris Worrell. James, who was gay, found himself falling in love. He was surprised to find out that Chris was in jail for rape, but didn't worry about it.

When both of them were free, they continued their friendship. James was in love, but knew that Worrell would never return his feelings. In fact, what Worrell liked best was to drive around Adelaide, picking up girls. James wasn't jealous. He even drove the car. He would drive them somewhere quiet and go for a walk while Chris was with the girl he'd picked up that night.

One evening, they picked up a young woman called Veronica Knight. When James returned from his walk, she was dead. James was shocked, but helped to bury her.

If he had reported this murder, six other women would have lived and he wouldn't have gone to prison. But his love and weakness won. He continued to drive Chris on his pickups – and continued to help him bury his victims.

In 1978, a man picking mushrooms in the Truro area found what was left of Veronica Knight. The police started to search the area and, over a year, found the remains of other girls who had gone missing between Christmas 1976 and February 1977: Sylvia Pittman, Vicki Howell, Connie Iordanides, Julie Mykyta, Tania Kenny and the last, Deborah Lamb, who had probably been still alive when Worrell buried her.

The disappearances had stopped some time ago, so the detectives decided that the murderer was probably in jail.

He wasn't in jail. He was dead. Not long after the murder of Deborah Lamb, Chris, James and a friend called Debbie went away for the weekend. Chris was in a bad mood and insisted on driving, even though he was drunk. The car crashed. Only James survived.

Chris Worrell had had a girlfriend, Amelia, who knew nothing about what he'd been doing. She was very sad about his death. One day, James made the mistake of telling her the truth about Chris.

However Amelia felt about this, she promised not to tell anyone. After all, Chris was dead and James hadn't actually killed anyone. What was the point?

But the bodies began to turn up. Then there was a reward of $30,000 offered for information. Whatever her reason for telling, Amelia finally told the police, who took James to the station for questioning.

At first, he denied everything, but eventually, he admitted to having been with Chris during the murders. He offered to show the police where the bodies had been buried.

In February 1980, three years after the last murder, James Miller went on trial. He argued that he was innocent because he hadn't actually killed the victims. He said he hadn't realised what was going to happen. These arguments didn't help him. He was acquitted of the murder of Veronica Knight, because he couldn't have known that would happen. As far as the judge was concerned, however, anyone who'd hang around while people were being killed,

not once but six times, was as guilty as if he had killed them himself.

Miller went back to jail, this time for life, though a few years later he managed to get a minimum sentence. This means he will eventually be released, though not till he is 74 years old. He has spent his time in prison complaining, going on hunger strikes and even writing a book about his innocence. What he has never done publicly is say he is sorry.

DID YOU KNOW...?

In 2008, Mark 'Chopper' Read was told he had only a few years to live, unless he had a life-saving liver transplant. Read refused because he felt that he didn't deserve it and that a liver transplant would be better given to some innocent child than to himself. After the story appeared in the newspapers, there was a flood of letters from readers, offering support, money, even transplant organs. Australians love an honest bad guy.

RAYMOND BENNETT
THE GREAT BOOKIE ROBBERY

Raymond Bennett was a career criminal. When he planned a robbery, it ran smoothly. It worked. He could probably have had a career in the army, as a commando leader. But crime paid a lot better.

While he was serving a prison term in England, Raymond began to plan the most daring robbery ever. Late in 1975, while he was still in jail, Raymond was allowed out on leave.

Other people would have taken a local holiday. Raymond climbed on a plane, came home to Melbourne and checked out the Victorian Club in Queen Street. Convinced that his idea would work, Raymond got back on the plane and returned to England to finish his sentence and plan his crime.

The Victorian Club had been around for nearly a century. During that time, after every major racing event, bookmakers, who made their living taking bets, would gather to 'settle up', or pay and receive money owed. Millions of dollars changed hands on those days. No one was expecting a robbery. The money was brought there in an armoured car. Police would visit to make sure everything was all right. Criminals assumed that it would be too hard to get in.

Little did they know how easy it actually was.

When Raymond got back to Melbourne, he chose his team and took them out to the bush to train. He made them promise to avoid drink and women for three months before the heist. Raymond couldn't afford to take a chance on anyone talking. It had to run quickly and smoothly. When he decided to do the job just after Easter – on 21 April 1976 – he took the team into the deserted building to rehearse over the weekend.

After Easter was the best time, because there would be money from three races, belonging to 116 bookmakers. The robbers would make a fortune!

The operation was embarrassingly easy. Just after noon, one of the team entered the building disguised as a repairman, supposedly to fix a fridge. Only seven minutes later, the team burst in, wearing balaclava masks, made the bookies lie on the floor and escaped with the money. They jammed the service lift with the empty cash boxes. It took just eleven minutes, including the time it took to get the money up the stairs to the office in the same building which they had rented before the robbery! While police hunted for the money and followed up leads about a white van, the money was right under their noses.

Afterwards, the police had an impossible time, trying to track the cash. They couldn't even find out how much money had been stolen, because many of those bookmakers didn't keep accurate records. This avoided paying some taxes. The official amount was $1.4 million, but it was probably a lot more than that, perhaps as much as $7 million.

Raymond made sure that his team didn't just go off and spend their loot. That would have made it easy for police to track them. The money was spread out. Some of it was invested in property, some went out of the country. There was so much that they had to find all sorts of ways to hide it. When Raymond's mother fainted one day, the ambulance officers found $90,000 hidden in her clothes!

Police had guessed Raymond was involved, but couldn't prove it. They tried to get information from his friend, Norman Lee, but Norman was no help to them at all, even after he was arrested for being involved in the robbery. Police had to release him, though, because they couldn't prove the money he had was from that particular robbery.

The police gave up. It seemed that Raymond and his friends had got away with the crime.

However, while nobody went to prison for this particular crime, all the robbers ended up suffering in other ways, because none of them could settle down and enjoy the money.

In November 1979, Raymond was waiting outside the Melbourne Magistrate's Court to go on trial for another robbery when a gunman who has never been definitely identified simply shot him dead.

That was the end of the leader of the Great Bookie Robbery.

DID YOU KNOW...?

In 1788, an eleven-year-old girl called Mary Wade was transported to Australia for luring a younger girl into the toilets, where she and another girl stole the poor child's underwear. She wasn't sorry at all, saying afterwards that she wished she had thrown her victim down the toilet! In Australia, Mary later married another convict and had 21 children. She would have been pleased to know that one of her descendants, Kevin Rudd, would become Prime Minister of Australia.

GEOFFREY CHAMBERS
AND KEVIN BARLOW

When Geoffrey Chambers was growing up in Perth, he dreamed of being famous one day. He would certainly become well-known, but not in the way he had hoped.

Geoffrey started his criminal career early, stealing and selling lawnmowers when he was only eleven years old. By 1977, as a young man, he was selling drugs on a small scale.

But Geoffrey Chambers wanted a nice house, fast

cars and all the other enjoyable things that money could buy – and he was a heroin user himself. Heroin was an expensive drug.

He began to buy heroin from Thailand and to sell it all over Australia. For a while, he had a Thai girlfriend who helped him, but she was sent back to Thailand as an illegal migrant. She stayed in touch, though, and continued to help him commit his crimes.

Chambers' next girlfriend was a trainee nurse called Sue. He introduced her to heroin and the two of them travelled to Asia quite often, bringing back illegal drugs. They were doing well and had a nice house by the sea, but they were worried about the police and decided to move to Sydney, travelling by car. On the way, the car crashed and Sue was killed.

Chambers was depressed. He didn't care much what happened to him after that. He drank far too much and took drugs.

In August 1983, he took a drug-smuggling trip to Penang in Malaysia for a drug boss called Paul Musarri. He was supposed to hand over the drugs to two other Australians whom he was to meet there, but he kept some of the heroin, burying it near his hotel.

The Australian police knew about the drug smugglers, though not about Chambers. Back in Australia, the pair were arrested. Paul Musarri was also in trouble.

Musarri desperately needed the money from the buried heroin. He asked Chambers to fetch it, but Chambers would need someone to help him. Kevin Barlow was boarding with a woman called Debbie whose boyfriend, John Asciak, was working with Musarri. Barlow seemed like a good person to ask, as he needed some money to pay off his car, which he was about to lose. He agreed to go, even though Debbie begged him not to.

From the very beginning, the two men made mistakes. They weren't supposed to travel together, as doing so would put them in more danger, but they did. They certainly weren't supposed to spend any of the money, but they did. Chambers and Barlow spent their first week in Malaysia drinking and using drugs. Making more mistakes was inevitable.

When the time came to smuggle the heroin, Barlow became nervous. The plan was that Chambers and Barlow would hide the drugs in their bodies. This was unpleasant, but a common way of smuggling drugs. If Barlow had followed the plan, perhaps they wouldn't have been caught. But he refused. In the end, they hid the drugs in their luggage.

At Penang airport, their drugs were found and they were arrested.

Now they were in real trouble. In Malaysia, drug smugglers were hanged.

Australians were shocked. No one in Australia had been executed since Ronald Ryan's hanging in the 1960s. And these two men were small criminals compared to those who had sent them. While they were in Penang prison, using heroin supplied by guards, the Australian government tried hard to get their sentences reduced. A National Crime Authority officer even visited John Asciak, who was in prison for another crime, to ask him to give evidence that would help keep the men from hanging, but he refused.

On 7 July 1986, after two years in prison, and in spite of a huge public outcry in Australia, the two drug smugglers were hanged. Geoffrey Chambers and Kevin Barlow were the first Westerners to be executed in Malaysia for drug offences.

DID YOU KNOW...?

An old pensioner called Billy Mears died in 2002, too poor to afford a tombstone. In 1949, Billy had escaped from jail with a more famous crook, Darcy Dugan. Among Billy's belongings, the minister from Sydney's Wayside Chapel found a lottery ticket which had won enough money to buy the tombstone.

DAVID AND CATHERINE BIRNIE

The story of the Birnies of Perth is a strong warning against ever accepting a lift from strangers, even if they look like a nice young couple.

Both David and Catherine Birnie had miserable childhoods. Neither of them had many friends, but they fell in love early, when they were both fifteen. They were jailed when they were eighteen, for housebreaking, but David kept committing crimes – 21 over five years. Catherine's parole officer told her that she and David were no good for each other and advised her to break up with him.

For a while, Catherine took this advice. She got a job and married her boss's son. They had several children together.

However, in 1985, Catherine left her husband and children to live with David. She changed her surname to Birnie. They moved into a house at 3 Moorhouse Street in Willagee. David got a job at a car wrecker's in April 1986.

Later that year, women started disappearing. The first was Mary Neilson, a university student who vanished one day in October when she went to buy some tyres for her car.

Susannah Candy, a high school student, disappeared a couple of weeks later. She was forced to write her parents two letters saying she was safe.

Denise Brown, a computer operator, went missing on her way home from a friend's house. She phoned home to say she was okay, but her friends worried anyway – with good reason.

The fourth victim was Noelene Patterson, a former flight attendant, who was working at the Nedlands Golf Club. She went missing on 30 October, but her disappearance wasn't reported until several days later, after the Birnies had been caught.

On 10 November, a half-naked teenage girl ran into a shopping complex, begging for help. She told police that she had been kidnapped at knifepoint by a couple, while giving them directions. They had driven her to their house and chained her to the bed. The man had raped her twice. They had forced her to ring home, saying she was safe. The girl had escaped when the man was at work and the woman went to answer the door. She gave a good description of the house.

The police found the Birnies' house easily enough. They searched it and found some evidence, but needed more. They decided to question them separately, in hope that one of them would break down and confess.

It didn't take long for them to get confessions, first from David, then from Catherine. At 7.00 p.m., the Detective Sergeant said, 'It's getting dark. Best we take the shovel and dig them up'.

To his amazement, David agreed. 'Okay,' he said. 'There's four of them.'

The first grave was Denise Brown's; she had accepted a lift. After David had abused her, they took her to a pine plantation, where he did it again, while Catherine held a torch. Then he stabbed his victim. Killing her was harder than they thought. A larger knife also didn't kill her so finally they hit her on the head with an axe.

Mary Neilson, their first victim, had made the

mistake of trying to buy tyres from David, whom she had met at the car wrecker's. She had been buried in the Gleneagles National Park, after David strangled her with a nylon strap.

Susannah Candy had been hitchhiking. This time, David asked Catherine to do the killing, as proof of her love for him. Catherine strangled the girl.

The last grave was that of Noelene Patterson, who'd been unlucky enough to run out of petrol when the Birnies were passing. Catherine spat on this one. David hadn't wanted to kill this victim, making Catherine jealous. Catherine had insisted, so he'd given their victim sleeping tablets and strangled her while she slept.

Both David and Catherine were sentenced to 'strict security life imprisonment'. This meant that they couldn't get parole for twenty years. From their separate jails, they exchanged thousands of letters.

David Birnie killed himself in 2005. Catherine is unlikely ever to be released.

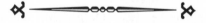

DID YOU KNOW...?

During World War II, night time street lighting was reduced, to make it harder for the enemy to bomb cities. This was known as 'brownout'. Unfortunately, it wasn't only the enemy who were a problem. And if brownout made bombing harder, it made murder easier. American soldier Eddie Leonski was stationed in Melbourne, where he continued his drinking binges. Leonski had been in trouble before, trying to strangle a woman in America. He drank a lot and became violent. In May 1942, he used the brownout to commit three murders, all of women older than himself. He was caught when a soldier he'd confided in reported him. During his trial, Leonski didn't explain why he committed murder. He only said of one of his victims, 'I wanted that voice. I choked her'. Despite this, he was found sane and was executed in November 1942.

JOHN WAYNE GLOVER
THE GRANNY KILLER

In 1989, a number of older women were attacked in the expensive Sydney suburb of Mosman. Some survived. Most didn't.

At first, police thought the killer must be a young man, perhaps even a boy who had issues with his grandmother.

One man, Raymond Roper, was attacked from behind, while he was wearing a long coat and a floppy straw hat. When he turned to defend himself, the attacker, realising he was a man, ran away. Raymond said his attacker was about 30, with blond hair, so police started looking for someone young. Just in case, they also considered teenagers.

That was a mistake.

The first victim, 84-year-old Gwendoline Mitchelhill, was hit on the head outside her home in March 1989. Strangely, her shoes had been taken off and laid neatly by her head.

This became a 'signature' of the killer.

The next victim, Lady Winifreda Ashton, 84, died in the bin room of her unit block. Her shoes, hat and handbag had been laid neatly next to her walking stick.

Someone truly sick was at work – but who?

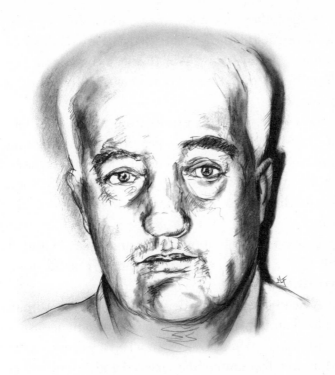

Police continued to check out local schools and watch for a young man.

The next victim, Doris Cox, survived, but couldn't identify her attacker. She did remember being startled by a young skateboarder. This seemed to support the police's theory about the killer's youth.

But the attacker wasn't young. He was a 58-year-old pie salesman, John Glover, who lived with his wife, two children and in-laws.

John Glover wasn't young, but he did have issues with older women. His mother, Freda, had left him with his father and taken his younger brother with her. Even before she left, she was not a good influence on him. During World War II, she had made money illegally. She even burned down her own shop for the insurance.

Glover arrived in Australia from Britain in 1956, at first living in Melbourne, occasionally getting into trouble with the law. Then he met and married Sydney woman Gay Rolls. They moved to Sydney. His mother-in-law, Essie, made it clear she didn't like him.

However he felt about Freda and Essie, he didn't kill them. Instead, he took his anger out on other older women.

A year before the murders started, he met a woman called Joan Sinclair and they began a romance.

In January 1989, Glover attacked a woman called Margaret Todhunter. She survived and described her attacker. For a long time, no one made a connection between the grey-haired man in a suit and tie she described and the young thug police were hunting. Another survivor, 82-year-old Euphemia Carnie, gave a description a lot like Margaret Todhunter's.

Now the police began to wonder: could their man be older than they had thought?

In early November, Glover killed two women in as many days, Margaret Pahud and Olive Cleveland. Next, a woman called Muriel Falconer was bashed over the head in her own hallway. This time, Glover left a helpful footprint in the blood around the body.

An old woman he attacked in bed at the Greenwich Hospital pressed an alarm button. A nurse called the police, who suspected him, but hadn't enough evidence to hold him. They decided to keep an eye on him.

Glover tried to commit suicide. He left a suicide note for his family, saying there would be no more grannies. He survived that suicide attempt. The police found the note, but, for some reason, didn't do anything with it.

On 19 March, Glover decided to kill Joan Sinclair, then himself. It didn't occur to the police watching her house that he might be planning to murder his girlfriend. After a few hours, however, they entered Joan's home. She was dead, bashed over the head. John Glover was in the bath with Scotch and tablets, just about to slip under the water.

He was convicted of six counts of murder and sentenced to life in prison. There were six more murders which police believed he had committed, but they couldn't be sure.

His family never went to see him and in 1992, his wife said he would be better off dead.

In 2005, John Glover was found dead in his prison cell, where he was thought to have killed himself. He'd finally succeeded in committing suicide.

JULIAN KNIGHT
HODDLE STREET MASSACRE

From an early age, Julian Knight, the Hoddle Street killer, was fascinated by guns and death. A schoolmate later said he brought more than 100 photos of dead bodies to school to show the other students. It was said that he enjoyed describing in detail how bullets had damaged the bodies. Graffiti he had scribbled on his textbooks showed a disturbingly racist attitude.

In January 1987, he started officer training at the Royal Military College, Duntroon, but he didn't last long. He wasn't very good at anything except the weapons-based subjects. When he stabbed his sergeant at a Canberra nightclub, he was asked to leave the army for good. His trial for assault and malicious wounding was supposed to take place in June, but was postponed to November.

If he had been tried and jailed in June, perhaps the Hoddle Street tragedy would never have happened, but by November, police had a lot more to worry about than one fight in a nightclub. Julian Knight was back in Melbourne. He had killed seven people and injured nineteen more.

What made him decide to gather all those bullets and guns on the evening of 9 August 1987, and go on a random shooting spree? And why Hoddle Street, anyway? He wasn't after his enemies. He wasn't trying to get revenge on anyone. The people he killed didn't know him. They were just there.

Years later, the policeman who had questioned him right after the crime said that Julian had been happy and excited after the killings. He had bragged about what he had just done. It was fun, for him.

All we know is that he left home at 9.29 p.m. and that a minute later he was shooting at people.

He shot a woman who had got out of her car – six times, till she was dead. Then he shot two people who came to help her. Three more people died in the next few minutes. He kept shooting at anyone passing on the street and then at police. He shot at a police car and then at a police helicopter, forcing it to land. Finally, after a chase through the streets of Melbourne's suburbs, police managed to catch him in Fitzroy North, just before 10.15 p.m.

At this time, Victorian law didn't allow a life sentence without parole. Also, Julian was only nineteen. That meant, as a young offender, he had to have a chance to reform. He was sentenced to a minimum of 27 years. He could apply for parole in 2014.

In jail, he was allowed to further his education. The idea was that it would make him a better person when he left. Unfortunately, the education he chose was not one that suggested he was planning to go straight when he left jail. In 2001, he had finished a degree in military strategy and weapons – at taxpayers' expense!

Over the years, he also went to court many times

to complain. He didn't like being in a high-security prison. He was angry when he got into trouble for having sharp things in his cell and computer disks with information about the prison staff. He considered it an abuse of his human rights when they took away his Ku Klux Klan and Nazi collections.

In 2004, after he had spent about $250,000 worth of taxpayers' money on his many complaints, he was declared a vexatious litigant – someone who was wasting time and money on silly protests. He was not allowed to take any more legal action in Victoria for ten years, except with special permission.

In 2007, he complained that the prison authorities were interfering with his rehabilitation when they wouldn't allow him to send a letter of apology to a victim. He wanted to be gradually moved to lower-security prisons and have access to programs that would help him after release.

Unless he has changed a lot, it's unlikely his wish will be granted in the near future.

THE SIGMA BREAK-IN

It was like something out of a Hollywood thriller. The team of burglars had been practising for months. They had been checking out various chemical companies in Victoria and South Australia and decided on a Melbourne company called Sigma.

Sigma made drugs to treat such problems as ADD (Attention Deficit Disorder, a behaviour problem suffered mostly by young boys), but the ingredients could be used to make speed, a dangerous street drug that would be worth a fortune to the robbers. George Lipp, Paul Elliott, Brian Zerma and Mark Wills weren't professional criminals. They just wanted to be rich.

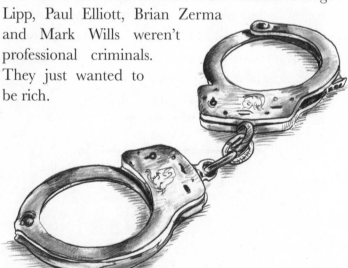

There were two factories in Melbourne's southeast, one in Clayton, the other in Croydon. They were going to merge and there wasn't much time for the burglary to be carried out. The burglars broke in 25 times over the nine months before the real thing. During these practice runs, they looked up the company's records to see what was in the safe. They checked the security systems and found their way around the huge complex. They had $30,000 worth of equipment to help them in their heist.

What they didn't have was someone who knew how to get into the safe where the containers of drugs were kept.

Lipp remembered a man he used to know in the early 1980s who worked in the security industry. He was an expert on safes. Let's call him 'Fred'.

One night in August 1996, Lipp visited the safe expert. First he asked him if he could help open a safe for his mother, who'd lost her key. Fred agreed and went with him. After he'd opened it, Lipp asked him if he could open a much more complicated safe. He showed him a photo of what was obviously not a home safe. He offered him $100,000 to open it.

Fred knew he'd been asked to help with a robbery. To give himself time, he asked for a clearer picture of the safe. Next day, he told Chris Gyngell, the state manager of Chubb Security, what had happened. Gyngell rang the police drug squad.

But they couldn't just arrest the burglars. They had

to catch them in the act. There was an undercover agent, 'Dave', who would be able to take over as the safebreaker, but Fred had to introduce him.

Chubb Security gave Dave a crash course in safe-breaking. He would have to convince the burglars that he knew what he was doing.

Fred rang Lipp and pretended to be interested in the robbery. Lipp met him in a pub and discussed the matter. It soon became clear that he wanted the expert to come with them on the night and actually open the safe. Even when he introduced Dave, Lipp wasn't interested unless Fred also came along.

It was going to be horribly dangerous for the civilian, but it was the only way.

The two undercover men recorded a number of planning sessions, to incriminate the burglars later.

On 15 September, police set up a surveillance team near the factory. They had put secret cameras in the vault room, where the safe was kept.

Now the thriller started to look more like a comedy. The robbers had planned to put their own cameras in the room, because they'd seen a movie about this sort of heist, *Heat* with Robert de Niro, and were copying what the fictional thieves had done. It had to work! When they found the police cameras, instead of running, they were merely annoyed that someone had got in before them.

On the big night, Paul Elliott gave everyone in the team the equipment they needed. He also gave them stopwatches. They didn't really have any use for the stopwatches, but the characters in *Heat* had them, so they would too.

Lipp and Elliott broke in and disabled the security system. They came out and called the two safecrackers to do their part of the job. It was a wet and miserable night and there were a lot of accidents happening on the slippery roads. The heist took four hours, as they waited for various emergency vehicles to go past. Finally, they came out and the police pounced.

The four men went on trial in October 1998 and pleaded guilty. They all received a number of years in prison, although Elliott's defence told the court that he'd been trying hard to rehabilitate himself while he was out on bail. He'd got himself a job.

He was working for a security alarm company.

DID YOU KNOW...?

In 1929, Lewis Lasseter, a man who had tried a number of careers and not done too well in any of them, wrote to the member for Kalgoorlie, A.E. Green, telling him that he'd discovered a vast, gold-bearing reef in Central Australia, eighteen years before. He was ignored. Next, Lasseter spoke to John Bailey of the Australian Workers Union. He told Bailey he'd found the reef 33 years before! The Depression was on. The idea of all that gold was tempting. Bailey listened. An expedition set out from Alice Springs in July 1930. They found nothing and most of them turned back. Lasseter kept going and died. It's thought now that he got the idea from some novels popular at the time. Certainly, he'd never been to Central Australia before. Oddly enough, there are still people who believe in 'Lasseter's Reef'.

PETER DUPAS
SERIAL KILLER

Peter Dupas committed his first violent crime in 1968, when he was only fifteen. He asked a neighbour to lend him a knife for peeling vegetables and then stabbed her with it. She survived the attack and Peter told police he didn't know why he'd done it.

That time, he only got probation and psychiatric treatment.

Over the next few years, Dupas spent time in jail for several more attacks on women.

Every time Dupas came out of jail for one offence, he would commit another. Despite this, he often didn't serve full terms for his crimes.

The first murder for which Dupas was jailed was the last he actually committed. Evidence for two others turned up after he was already behind bars.

Nicole Patterson was a youth counsellor. She had a job working for the Ardoch Youth Foundation, but she wanted to do some private work from her home in the Melbourne suburb of Northcote. In 1999, she advertised in the local newspapers and had a call from someone who told her his name was Malcolm. She made an appointment and wrote it into her diary, along with a mobile phone number.

On the morning of 19 April, neighbours heard screams coming from her house. Later that day, a friend coming to take her to dinner found her mutilated body. She had been stabbed 27 times. Her breasts had been cut off. They were missing. So was the murder weapon.

Police checked the mobile phone number in Nicole's diary. The phone belonged to someone else, who let them know Peter Dupas' name.

Dupas had been planning the murder carefully. He'd phoned Nicole three times, supposedly to arrange counselling, but really to find out how easy it would be to kill her. Police found plenty of evidence at his home. There was bloodstained clothing, tape similar to tape found on the victim's body, a balaclava, her ad from the local paper and clippings about the murder.

The jury took less than three hours to find him guilty. He was sentenced to life imprisonment.

While he was in jail, evidence turned up for other murders which had been unsolved until then.

A woman called Margaret Maher had been murdered in October 1997, in the suburb of Broadmeadows. A man found her body under a cardboard box. Her breasts, like Nicole's, had been cut off. There was a black glove found near the body which turned out to have Dupas' DNA on it.

The trial for this murder, in 2004, went for three weeks. Again, Dupas was found guilty and sentenced

to life imprisonment. The jury didn't know he was already in prison for another murder.

Only a month after the murder of Margaret Maher, Mersina Halvagis went to visit her grandmother's grave at Melbourne's Fawkner Cemetery. Her fiancé found her body. She had been stabbed 87 times, mostly around the breasts.

Dupas, who was already in prison for the other crimes, was not convicted right away, even though many witnesses said they had seen him at the cemetery that day. His defence lawyer argued that he was suspected just because he lived nearby and he'd been in trouble for violent crimes before. That didn't mean he'd done it this time.

But there was a breakthrough late in 2006. A man called Andrew Fraser had known him in the Port Phillip Prison in 2002. He said that while they were gardening one day, they had found a homemade knife. Dupas had held it, murmuring, 'Mersina, Mersina…' When another prisoner had accused him of murdering her, he'd asked Andrew Fraser, 'How did he know I did it?' And he had spoken of it over several months.

At the trial in 2007, it took the jury just over a day to find him guilty again. A third life sentence was added to the other two.

Peter Dupas is suspected of three more murders. Whether or not he is convicted of those, he will not be leaving prison alive.

MARTIN BRYANT
PORT ARTHUR MASSACRE

It was 28 April, a beautiful autumn afternoon in 1996. In the former penal colony of Port Arthur, Tasmania, tourists were enjoying the sunshine. The Broad Arrow Cafe was full of people having lunch and browsing in the gift shop. Nobody could have guessed that in a short time, 35 people would be dead and 37 others injured.

A young blond man entered the cafe, carrying a sports bag. After eating lunch, he put the bag onto a table. He took out a video camera, then pulled out a semi-automatic rifle and began to shoot people, beginning with a Malaysian couple, Ng Moh Yee William and Chung Soo Leng. Within fifteen seconds, he had shot twelve people. He didn't know these people or care. He just wanted to shoot someone. Plenty of someones.

In eight minutes, he had murdered twenty people in the cafe and gift shop before moving on to the car park.

Outside, the man, whose name was Martin Bryant, shot some more people, including some tourists in – and under – a bus. A woman called Nanette Mikac had come to Port Arthur for a picnic with her two daughters while her husband was playing golf. Now

Bryant shot her and her younger daughter, Madeline. Alannah, the elder daughter, ran away, but Martin Bryant chased her down and shot her, too. He continued his shooting spree from his car, then shot the owners of another car before stealing it. Finally, he held up a white Toyota, shot the female driver and forced the man into the boot of the car, driving the car on to a guesthouse called the Seascape. There, he dragged his hostage inside, where the bodies of the owners, David and Sally Martin, lay. He had killed them on his way to Port Arthur.

By this time, someone had contacted the police, but because Bryant had a hostage, they didn't dare rush the house. They called in expert negotiators, who spoke to him for several hours until his phone batteries ran out. The next morning, he started a fire and ran out, his clothes burning. He surrendered to the police, who took him to hospital to have his burns treated. The police found the dead bodies of his hostage and the Martins.

Who was Martin Bryant and why did he do this terrible thing?

Martin was born in 1967. He was a strange boy who didn't get on with anyone at school. He preferred to be alone, and was often bullied when he wasn't terrifying people. He had a very low IQ, about 66, and didn't seem unhappy when his father's body was found drowned in a dam. The death was treated as suicide.

Martin's low intelligence meant that he was able to claim a pension when he left school instead of looking for work. However, he did odd jobs for a rich woman called Helen Harvey, who lived in a huge house in Hobart. They became great friends. Helen spent thousands of dollars on Martin. When she was killed in a car crash, she left Martin all her money and the big house. He enjoyed himself, travelling and spending money, but it seems this wasn't enough for him.

After the massacre, some people suggested that he couldn't possibly have known what he was doing, but it turned out that he had visited Port Arthur several times before the day of the murders. He had also measured the sports bag carefully when buying it. These clear plans suggest that he did know what he was doing.

We will never be really sure of his reasons behind what he did. He was considered fit to stand trial and in November 1996 he was sentenced to 35 life sentences, one for each person he had killed, to make sure he would never be released. For ten years,

Martin lived at Hobart's Risdon Prison. In 2006, after a number of suicide attempts, he was moved to a special mental health unit, to be treated by doctors and nurses.

This tragedy led to a change in Australia's gun laws and a ban on all semi-automatic weapons.

DID YOU KNOW...?

Con artist Murray Beresford Roberts once managed to steal some diamonds from a jewel dealer in India. Travelling to India, he posed as a rich British lord who was there at the time. Pretending he was shopping for a diamond coronet as an anniversary gift, he was introduced to a dealer, who trusted him with the coronet. Ripping the jewels out of the headpiece, he swallowed them and flew to London, where they - ugh! - came out at the other end and he cleaned and sold them. What happened when the real lord was presented with Murray's hotel and jewellery bill, we'll never know.

LUCY DUDKO

Lucy Dudko was in love. The Russian-born librarian had a new boyfriend, John Killick. John was a perfect gentleman who treated her well and brought her coffee in bed every morning. Even better, she thought, he was protecting her from her violent former husband. The pair had been living together for about a year in a place called Queanbeyan in New South Wales.

There was only one problem: John was a thief. He was a thief who had been caught committing armed robbery in 1998. When he was arrested and sentenced to several years in Sydney's Silverwater Prison, Lucy was horrified.

She decided that she wasn't going to take this disaster lying down. She didn't care what John had done. She loved him! She decided that she would free him, somehow.

Being a librarian, Lucy knew how to do research. She made her plans

147

carefully and borrowed some videos to help her carry them out. There were three videos about daring prison escapes – *The Getaway, Captive* and a Charles Bronson movie, *Breakout*, in which there was an exciting escape by helicopter.

This seemed like a wonderful idea. In March 1999, Lucy spent $360 on hiring a helicopter for a joyride over Sydney. She told pilot Tim Joyce that she wanted to take a look at the site of the Olympic Games, which were going to happen the following year.

Poor Tim! How could he have imagined, when he left for work that morning, that he would suddenly find a gun being pointed at him by an excitable Russian woman, demanding that he take her to the yard of the maximum security Silverwater Prison? Being hijacked was bad enough, but when the helicopter arrived at the jail, Tim found himself being shot at!

The couple made him take them to a park near Macquarie University, where they argued as to whether or not they should keep him as a hostage. In the end, they tied him to a tree and escaped together.

For the next 45 days, the newspapers were full of their adventures. The hunt for them was on. To the annoyance of the police, many people actually hoped that Lucy and John would escape. However, their luck finally ran out in early May when they were found in a caravan park, registered as Mr and

Mrs Brown. John was taken back to prison and had an extra fifteen years added to his sentence.

Lucy was sentenced to ten years in jail, though she protested she was innocent and that someone else had hijacked the helicopter. Unfortunately for her, those videos were found in her home.

During her time in prison, she continued to protest her innocence, even appealing to the UN Commission for Human Rights in Geneva. Nothing helped. And jail wasn't that bad. Even her father in Moscow said that if she had to go to jail, she was much better off in an Australian prison than a Russian one! Lucy became a model prisoner and was released in 2006, after serving seven of her ten years.

Perhaps she wishes she had returned those videos to the library on time.

IVAN MILAT
BACKPACKER MURDERS

etween 1989 and 1992, seven young hitchhikers were bashed, strangled, stabbed and shot. Their bodies were dumped in Belanglo State Forest, outside Sydney.

Ivan Milat, their killer, was one of fourteen children. His parents couldn't handle him. He left school at fourteen, and was soon in trouble with the law, spending a total of about five years in jail by the time he was 25. He married, but his wife left him, suspecting there was

something not quite right about him. He frightened her.

Late in 1989, two young university students from Melbourne, Deborah Everist and James Gibson, went to Sydney for a holiday. Deborah rang her mother from Sydney to say they were fine, but that was the last time they ever spoke. She and James went south along the Hume Highway, towards Albury. Then they vanished.

A month later, Paul Onions, a British backpacker, was on his way to Mildura. He accepted a lift. Outside the city, the driver pulled out a gun. Paul escaped from the car, leaving his belongings behind. He stopped a car and urged the driver, Joanne Berry, to drive on. Joanne later identified the 4WD and its driver.

She dropped Paul off at the local police station, where he told his story. He and Joanne were both witnesses in Milat's trial.

A year later, German tourist Simone Schmidl was on her way to Melbourne to meet her mother. She told friends she was planning to hitchhike. They said it was unsafe and offered to pay her fares. But Simone insisted on hitching.

She disappeared.

On Boxing Day 1991, two German students, Gabor Neugebauer and Anja Habschied, left Sydney and also vanished.

Tourists Joanne Walters and Caroline Clarke left

Sydney on 18 April 1992, never to be seen alive again, except by their killer.

In September 1992, two bushwalkers found Joanne Walters' body. They contacted police, who soon found Caroline Clarke's remains. Both girls had died horribly. Caroline's head had been used for target practice. Police also found cartridges from a gun called a 10/22 Ruger.

What was left of university students James and Deborah was discovered in October 1993 in the same region.

Police began to search the Belanglo Forest for other bodies.

Simone Schmidl's body turned up on 1 November. She had been stabbed several times. Finally, they unearthed the bones of Gabor and Anja. Anja's skull was missing.

One hundred cartridge cases from bullets used by the killer were found around these bodies. There was also the wrapping from Winchester .22 calibre bullets. It had the batch number on it.

Now, police investigators had to find the murder weapon itself. It wasn't easy, since there were 55,000 Ruger guns of that model listed in Australia. There were even more bullets from that batch. But somehow the police found the gun shop where Ivan Milat did his shopping.

Information poured in. Especially useful was one woman's mention of a certain Ivan Milat who liked guns and had a property near the forest. Paul Onions returned to Australia to be a witness. He identified Milat from a photo.

Police investigators watched Milat's home and questioned his family and workmates. His employers said he'd been off work on the days when the murders happened. Now nervous, Milat asked his brother Wally to hide most of his guns for him.

But when police started raiding properties they suspected might contain evidence, they got enough evidence to arrest Ivan Milat on 22 May 1994. In his house were guns, including a murder weapon, and ammunition matching what they'd found in the forest. They even found some of the victims' camping equipment. The DNA retrieved from a blood-covered cord matched Caroline's. At Wally Milat's home, they found most of Ivan's guns and literally a tonne of ammunition.

No matter how much evidence was piled up against him, Ivan insisted he had been framed. But 170 witnesses and hundreds of statements and photos said otherwise.

On 20 July 1996, a jury found him guilty of the seven murders and the attempted murder of Paul Onions. He was sentenced to life imprisonment. It is unlikely he will ever be released.

MARK BRANDON 'CHOPPER' READ

Unlike most criminals, Mark 'Chopper' Read has become a celebrity. Since leaving prison for the last time in 1998, he has been writing books, doing live stage performances, recording rap songs, acting and being interviewed about other criminals. In 2001, a film of his life was released, starring Eric Bana.

And yet, between the ages of 20 and 38, he was only out of prison for thirteen months!

Born in Melbourne, Chopper had a disturbed childhood. Amongst other things, he was taken from his parents at the age of fourteen.

By the time he turned fifteen, Chopper had his own gang. He robbed drug dealers and other crooks. Years later he explained that he picked on criminals because, after all, they weren't going to call the police.

In the late 1970s, Chopper actually managed to start a gang war in prison! He was in Pentridge Prison's high-security H-Division at the time. When he applied to get out of H-Division and was turned down, Chopper decided that he was going to get out of there somehow, even if it was only to hospital.

On request, another prisoner cut Chopper's ears

off. Cutting off ears was no big deal to Chopper; he'd done it to someone else at one stage, though not by request.

Pentridge was not a healthy place to be imprisoned. His own gang attacked him when they felt he was going too far, injuring him badly.

Outside prison, Chopper continued his criminal career. Even some of the criminals involved in Melbourne's gang wars were frightened of him. One of them, Alphonse Gangitano, even took his family and escaped to Italy when he heard that Chopper was about to finish his latest prison sentence in 1991. Chopper wasn't free for long and Gangitano came home, although maybe he shouldn't have. Someone else killed Alphonse in his own home in 1998.

Chopper was now in Tasmania's Risdon Prison, with a stamp on his file saying, 'Never to be released' as he was tagged a 'dangerous criminal'. He'd been imprisoned for shooting a bikie called Sidney Collins. Chopper had said he didn't do it, but he went to jail anyway.

Somehow, all that crime and prison time hadn't stopped him from writing books. His books even got him a wife. Mary-Anne Hodge, who worked for the Australian Tax Office, enjoyed his books so much that she went to visit him in jail in 1993. They married in 1995, when he was still never to be released, but in 1998 his 'dangerous criminal' tag was overturned and he was set free.

Chopper and Mary-Anne settled on a farm in Tasmania, where they had a son, Charlie.

By 2001, though, the marriage was over and Chopper returned to Melbourne, where he moved in with a new girlfriend, Margaret. Since he wasn't going back to his life of crime, Chopper made his living from being a celebrity who had been a criminal. His books sold in the hundreds of thousands. People were always interested in hearing what he had to say about life, the universe and everything.

Still, he has upset a lot of people. He turned up drunk for a TV interview. He wrote a children's book with a hero who committed murder. He said that his politics were somewhere to the right of Genghis Khan – in other words, very conservative. Many people don't think he should be allowed to make money, even indirectly, out of his life of crime.

Australians are still arguing over whether he is a likeable character or just another crook, and a violent one at that. Some have compared him to Ned Kelly.

Since people are still arguing about Ned Kelly after more than 100 years, perhaps it's not too bad a comparison.

DID YOU KNOW...?

In 1925, Perth girl Audrey Jacob shot her fiancé, Cyril, in front of witnesses. One night, when Cyril was supposed to be somewhere else, Audrey went to a ball. There was Cyril, dancing with another woman. Audrey went home, but returned, carrying a gun. When Cyril pretended not to recognise her, she shot him. The jury took two days to find her not guilty.

THE SNOWTOWN MURDERS

Snowtown is a tiny town north of the South Australian capital, Adelaide. Nobody would have expected the gruesome discovery that was made there in a disused bank vault in 1999.

The bodies of eight victims were found in plastic barrels of acid, along with the various tools that had been used to torture the victims. The final murder had been committed right in the building. The dead man was David Johnson, half-brother of James Vlassakis, one of the four to be tried for murder. Vlassakis had lured him there. The killers thought it would be a nice, quiet place where no one would ever notice. As it turned out, the fact that Snowtown was so quiet was why the bodies were found.

Three days later, two more bodies turned up in a backyard in the Adelaide suburb of Salisbury North. Altogether, there were eleven murders. Only four of the six people involved were alive to stand trial. One, Elizabeth Harvey, died of cancer. Another, Thomas Trevilyan, who had helped with one murder, became a victim himself.

The leader of the group was John Justin Bunting. Bunting didn't care why he killed. You could offend him by being fat, gay, a drug user – almost anything.

When he was a child, his favourite hobby was burning insects in acid. Later, he used acid to try dissolving human bodies. Nearly all of the victims were people who knew their killers. The murderers made nearly $95,000 by claiming their victims' pension money, but Bunting simply liked killing. Worse, he enjoyed torturing his victims before he killed them.

The others who were tried for murder were Robert Wagner, Mark Haydon and James Vlassakis, whose mother, Elizabeth Harvey, had helped with one of the murders. Haydon wasn't convicted of any of the murders, as the evidence was uncertain, but he did plead guilty to helping to get rid of the bodies.

The bodies in the yard of Bunting's house in Salisbury North were those of Suzanne Allen, a friend of Bunting's, and Ray Davies, a mentally disabled man who lived in a caravan behind her

yard. The killers later insisted that Allen had died of a heart attack.

In 1998, Bunting and Wagner killed Mark Haydon's wife, Elizabeth, in her home while her husband was out. Killing her was a mistake. Her brother wouldn't believe Mark Haydon's excuses for her disappearance. She would never have left without her two children. The police found it strange that her own husband hadn't reported her disappearance. They started to keep an eye on the suspects. They even bugged Mark Haydon's house.

The barrels were moved around to different places before finally being taken to the Snowtown vault that Haydon had rented under the name of Mark Lawrence.

Snowtown was not a good place to hide something you didn't want anyone to notice. Any stranger bringing barrels there to stash away in a vault was asking to have it checked out.

The police who found the bodies later described the place as something out of a nightmare. During the trials, three members of the jury were so sickened that they dropped out.

The trials went from 2001 to 2004, with some appeals happening in 2005. Vlassakis pleaded guilty to four murders and received a life sentence. In September 2003, Bunting was convicted of eleven murders and Wagner of seven. The judge sentenced them to imprisonment for life, never to be released.

After the discovery of the barrels, there was some sickening tourism. People wanted to go to Snowtown to see where the bodies had been kept. Some wanted to take a sniff at the bank vault, hoping to catch the stink of the bodies. Others took photos.

Someone suggested the town's name be changed to Rosetown, to get away from the embarrassing and unpleasant press the town's people had had to put up with. That suggestion was never taken up.

The house in Salisbury North was knocked down. Who, after all, could live there after what had happened?

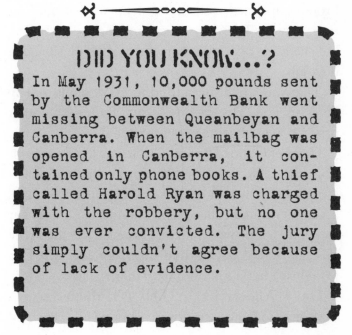

DID YOU KNOW...?

In May 1931, 10,000 pounds sent by the Commonwealth Bank went missing between Queanbeyan and Canberra. When the mailbag was opened in Canberra, it contained only phone books. A thief called Harold Ryan was charged with the robbery, but no one was ever convicted. The jury simply couldn't agree because of lack of evidence.

HEATHER PARKER
– PETER GIBB

Heather Parker, a prison guard at the Melbourne Remand Centre, wasn't very popular at work. Actually, she got on better with the prisoners than she did with the other guards – especially one prisoner, Peter Gibb, who was there for armed robbery.

In May 1992, she caused the other prison officers to go on strike after she was caught going into a broom cupboard with her new boyfriend! She was transferred to Pentridge prison and then to a hospital, but she wasn't popular there either. Finally, she got a desk job.

That was when she started to make plans to help Peter escape. His friend Archie Butterly, another prisoner, would come with him.

Heather planned it carefully. She ordered weapons from the United States. She got all the equipment the prisoners would need for a life on the run and asked a criminal called Alex Thompson to steal her a car and a four-wheel drive. However, she made the mistake of not paying him much for the job. This would cost her a lot more than money later.

On 7 March 1993, Gibb and Butterly used explosives to blow out a prison window. They escaped

in one of the stolen cars, with a prison officer called Donald Glasson chasing them in a taxi. Goodness knows what the taxi driver thought when he found himself going after escaped criminals.

Butterly and Gibb crashed the car, then a stolen motorbike. They shot Warren Treloar, a policeman who tried to stop them. Gibb grabbed Treloar's gun and the prisoners stole the police van. They abandoned the van when they met Heather in her own car. This was another mistake she made – at first, police thought she might have been kidnapped when they checked the number plates, but they weren't fooled for long.

In Frankston, the trio changed cars again, now using the stolen four-wheel drive. They drove out of Melbourne and stayed at a hotel in a small town called Gaffneys Creek, posing as a couple with a teenage son, who was staying in his room because he was sick. Heather and Peter went down to dinner and had an enjoyable evening with the other hotel guests. It was not a good idea because it meant people could describe them later. Still, they probably would have got away with it if the hotel hadn't burned down a few hours after they left. That brought the police out.

The police caught Heather and Peter on 13 March 1993. Archie Butterly was dead. Someone had shot him in the head, using Warren Treloar's gun. There was evidence that Heather might have done it, but she was never convicted of the crime.

During the trial, Alex Thompson said Heather had asked him to steal those cars, complaining about the 'lousy' $130 she had paid him.

Meanwhile, Heather sold her story both to the TV program *Sixty Minutes* and *Woman's Day* magazine. Police had to take the story from the magazine's offices. Heather was making money from her crime, which was against the law. Not only that, but the TV show and the magazine had made her look like a heroine who had done it all for love!

Her infatuation with Peter Gibb didn't impress the judge. He sentenced the pair to ten years in prison, but Heather's sentence was cut to five years and four months.

In 2007, she was in court again. She had attacked a woman whom she thought was competing with her for Peter Gibb's love. She didn't go back to jail, and Heather announced that she was considering breaking up with Peter anyway.

So ended the great love story.

DID YOU KNOW...?

In 2006, Queensland con artist Jody Harris was caught in Sydney, when someone recognised her. She pleaded guilty to 43 of 124 charges and was sentenced to four years in prison. Jody had 100 drivers' licences, various disguise items, a false passport and fake bank and Medicare cards. She is known as the 'Catch Me if You Can' thief, after another con artist in America who did similar things.

MATTHEW WALES
THE SOCIETY MURDERS

It was a cool evening in early April 2002. In their home in the Melbourne suburb of Glen Iris, Matthew Wales and his wife Maritza were preparing to entertain Matthew's mother, Margaret, and his stepfather, Paul King. While Maritza played with their two-year-old son, Domenik, Matthew was making dinner and setting the table. He had cooked a delicious vegetable soup.

Matthew, however, had added some ingredients not usually found in soup to Margaret and Paul's bowls. He had crushed a mixture of painkillers and blood pressure tablets, which he had heard made you sleepy.

Making his mother and stepfather sleepy was important to his plans. One other thing he had prepared was a piece of wood, which he had hidden in the front garden.

Dinner went well, though later Maritza said she had noticed that her husband's parents seemed a bit tired and her mother-in-law spoke in a strange way. However, she thought that perhaps Margaret had just drunk too much wine. Maritza did the dishes and took her little boy up to bed.

Matthew walked outside with his mother and

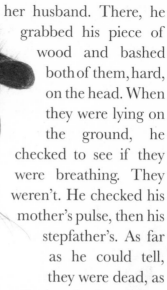

her husband. There, he grabbed his piece of wood and bashed both of them, hard, on the head. When they were lying on the ground, he checked to see if they were breathing. They weren't. He checked his mother's pulse, then his stepfather's. As far as he could tell, they were dead, as planned. When Maritza came downstairs, he told her what he had done, begging her not to tell on him.

Maritza was horrified. She pleaded with him to contact the police. When he wouldn't, she agreed not to call them, though she was unhappy. Maritza believed she should be loyal to her husband, whatever he had done. She was also afraid that Domenik would lose his father.

Matthew drove the car to Middle Park, where he left it. He hid the bodies in the garden under a pile of rubbish including a child's wading pool, and the next morning he hired a trailer and the equipment he needed to bury them. On Saturday, he drove to Marysville, a place 100 kilometres outside Melbourne, and buried the couple in a shallow grave.

By Sunday, the other members of Matthew's family were wondering what had happened to Margaret and Paul. Margaret was supposed to have lunch with Matthew's sister. She was never late and always told her family where she was. On Monday, the family told police that their parents were missing. Matthew said he had waved them goodbye on Thursday and had no idea where they were. Unhappily, Maritza supported him.

Unfortunately for Matthew, he made a lot of mistakes. He had tried to clean up, but police still found blood. He paid for everything with a credit card, which made it easier for police to work out what he had bought – and why. He thought he was burying the bodies in a lonely spot, but it was a popular camping place.

On 29 April, park rangers in Marysville found the bodies and soon afterwards Maritza told the police what she knew. Matthew was arrested and put on trial. Maritza was at first charged with being a part of the crime, but the charge was reduced to a two-year suspended sentence, since it was clear that she had known nothing about it. She had only lied to cover for him, slowing down the investigation of the crime.

Matthew admitted to his crime, but refused to accept that he had done anything wrong. He said that his mother had dominated his life and used money to control him. That wasn't what his brothers and sisters thought. Matthew had been the youngest child, only seven when his parents divorced, and had been spoiled rotten, they said.

The murders became known as the Society Murders because the victims were wealthy.

Matthew was convicted and sentenced to 30 years in prison.

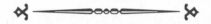

DID YOU KNOW...?

Mary Wade wasn't Kevin Rudd's only convict ancestor. In 2008, the Prime Minister was presented with a book that showed he had other convict ancestors. Thomas Rudd was transported to Australia in the nineteenth century for stealing a bag of sugar and married Mary Cable, who had stolen a bolt of cloth. One ancestor stole glue, while another female ancestor was transported in 1798 for forging coins. Perhaps Mr Rudd sometimes wishes he had her around when money is short...

SEF GONZALES

If your school marks were bad, you'd probably promise your parents to study harder and do better next time.

Sef Gonzales decided it was simpler just to kill his family before they found out.

Born in the Philippines, Sef came to Australia with his family in 1991, when he was eleven. His father Teddy, a lawyer, set up a business in Sydney. He and his wife Loiva worked hard and did well. They loved their two children, Sef and his sister Clodine, and wanted them to succeed in life. Sef was rather spoiled. He had money and designer clothes and, when he was old enough, his own car.

Sef was a strange boy, who could be violent. He also had an active imagination. He told his school friends that he had a recording contract, that he had cancer, that he had been shot at by a sniper. He also said that he was training for the Olympics, that he had a black belt in tae kwon do and even that he had a TV production company – anything his active imagination could come up with!

Sef's parents hoped he could become a doctor, but when he finished school, his marks weren't good enough. They persuaded him to do a special course which would let him study medicine later, but Sef failed again. After that, he did some subjects that would let him study law if he passed. But Sef was lazy. By 2001, it was looking as if he was going to fail that, too. He had to do something, before his family saw the letter with the bad news.

He would poison his mother, to start with. Sef didn't just slip something into her tea. He did his research, finding websites that told him what would work well, and ordered some poisonous castor oil seeds. Then he wrote anonymous letters to a food and drink company, saying their products had been poisoned so that they would take them off supermarket shelves. He hoped that the story would get into the newspapers and then, when his mother died, people would draw the wrong conclusion.

When the newspapers didn't report the story, he decided to go ahead with the murder anyway. His mother did become very ill, but she survived. Doctors didn't know why she had been sick. Disgusted, Sef threw out the seeds.

He'd just have to do this the hard way. Sef chose 10 July as the date for his mass murder. He gave himself an alibi by arranging to meet a friend for dinner. By the time he met his friend, the Gonzales family was already dead. They were all stabbed and Clodine was also hit with a baseball bat. Just to make it look good, he wrote a race hate message on the family room wall, signed KKK.

When he came home, he screamed that his family was dead and called in neighbours and the police,

claiming that he'd seen
someone running away.

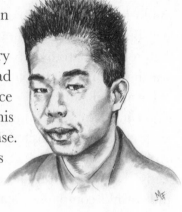

At first, people felt sorry
for the poor boy who had
lost his family, but the police
were never happy with his
story. It didn't make sense.
For one thing, the bodies
had been dead too long
to believe that someone
had hung around long
enough to be seen by Sef. And why had they used
knives from the kitchen to commit the murder? Also,
the paint used for the message matched some paint
kept in the garage.

But it was going to take time to gather enough
evidence against Sef, and he was allowed to go free
for the time being.

His relatives didn't believe his story either, not
even his grandparents, who left for Melbourne. If
they supported him, it was from a long way off!

Beginning to realise that he still might be caught,
Sef tried desperately to fix up his alibi, but only made
it worse. The evidence against him mounted up. Sef
was arrested in June 2002, nearly a year after the
murder, and sentenced to three life terms in prison.

The spoilt rich boy was never going to enjoy life
again.

JOE KORP AND TANIA HERMAN

In February 2005, Maria Korp, a mother of two, went missing. She was found after four days in the boot of her own car, near Melbourne's Shrine of Remembrance. The case became known as the 'Mum in the Boot' murder.

Joe Korp was Maria's second husband. After her first husband died in 1987, Maria met Joe at South Pacific Tyres, where they both worked.

The couple married in 1991. Later, Joe became fascinated with the Internet. He met a woman called Tania Herman on the Net. He told her his name was Joe Bronte and that he was single.

Tania lived in the town of Echuca, near the Murray River. In early 2004, Joe hired a car from Melbourne Airport and went to meet his new girlfriend. He told Maria that he had to go to Sydney on weekends to work on a new business with a friend.

Tania was planning to move to Melbourne, to be near her new lover. Joe decided he had to do something about Maria. He even checked out the cost of having her killed by a hit man.

Late in 2004, Maria found out about Tania. Angry, she left Joe's belongings outside the house for him to find when he came home. She had changed the locks. She asked the police for an intervention order, which meant that Joe couldn't come within 200 metres of her or the house. Later, he persuaded her to let him return to the family home.

Around that time, Joe and Tania started to think about how they might get rid of Maria. In January 2005, Joe asked Maria to help him with the car. She became suspicious about the tube, cloth and tape he asked her to fix to the car's exhaust. Maria was sure, now, that her life was in danger. She was right.

The murderous couple had decided that Tania would commit the actual deed. She would hide in Maria and Joe's garage, then strangle Maria. He put some equipment she would need into a backpack. She would even wear his running shoes so that her footprints would confuse police.

Early on the morning of 9 February 2005, Joe

picked up Tania and drove her to his home. He left her in the garage. After breakfast, he kissed Maria goodbye and left for work, only stopping to urge Tania not to let him down. She must kill Maria that day.

When Maria came out to her car, Tania tried to choke her with a belt, but there was a struggle between the two women and Maria bled on to the concrete before Tania finally managed to overcome her. She put Maria into her own car boot and drove to the Shrine, where she dumped the car. She took Maria's mobile phone, purse and car keys with her and threw the phone into the Yarra River.

Joe told the police his wife was missing. During the night, he found a spot of blood on the garage floor and tried to scrub it off with bleach. He took everything he thought might be evidence against them to Tania and told her to get rid of it all.

But some of the things they had tried to throw out turned up. It didn't take too much questioning by police to find that he had been involved with Tania. Both their homes were searched.

The car was still missing. Police asked the public to look out for it and on 13 February the car was found with Maria in the boot, still alive – just. She was taken to the Alfred Hospital.

Now Joe and Tania were suspected. They insisted they were innocent, but when police told Tania what they had found in her bin, she confessed.

In hospital, Maria was being fed artificially by tube, but she wouldn't recover. In late July, the feeding tube was removed. She died nine days later.

Joe had begun to feel guilty. Suddenly, he was grieving for the loss of Maria. After calling his first wife to share his grief, he hanged himself. Tania Herman went to prison, at least until 2014, regretting she'd ever been involved with Joe.

DID YOU KNOW...?

One day in 1919, Henry and Agnes Long were driving home along their local river bank. Suddenly they fell to the ground, dead. Both had been shot by one bullet, which had struck Henry in the neck, come out and hit Agnes in the right breast. It wasn't murder. A man shooting pelicans on the river had hit the unlucky couple when a shot ricocheted from the water.

NIKOLAI RADEV

When Bulgarian Nikolai Radev arrived in Australia in 1980, nobody bothered to ask him what he'd done back home. It was only later that his criminal background was found out.

Meanwhile, he was accepted as a refugee and soon settled into his new home in Melbourne. He married a nice girl called Sylvia and for a while he worked at an honest job, selling takeaway food in the suburbs.

By 1983, he wasn't working any more, but he was living the high life. It didn't take him long to find out who was running organised crime in Melbourne and join them. The Department of Immigration hadn't heard of him, but the Russian crooks in his new home certainly had.

By 1985, he'd spent his first jail time in Australia, for selling drugs. He didn't waste it. Criminals often see prison time as just a part of the job, and spend it learning new tricks and working on their next crime.

Nikolai's crimes were usually violent. Among other things, he had bashed an old man and tied up the man's little granddaughter. He even threatened one policeman who had arrested him; the policeman finally couldn't stand the pressure and quit his job.

By 1998, Radev had started selling drugs in St

177

Kilda, to help pay for the kind of life he liked to live. He paid in cash for the rent on a house in an expensive suburb of Melbourne. He wore expensive clothes and jewellery. His watch was worth $20,000 and work on his teeth had cost him $55,000. Just before his death, he bought himself a Mercedes for $100,000. Nobody without a job could live the way he did, except by crime.

It was Nikolai's greed that ended up killing him. He was making a lot of money from selling drugs, but this wasn't good enough for him. He wanted his own drugs 'cook', who would make pills for him all day, every day.

In 2003, he made the mistake of asking fellow drug dealer Carl Williams if he would introduce him to his cook.

Williams invited Radev to a meeting with other drug dealers at a café in Brighton. There, Nikolai was told the good news: the cook was in Coburg, another Melbourne suburb, and he would be allowed to meet him.

Happily, Radev got into his car and went to Coburg. Williams and his friends followed in two other cars. He reached Coburg and spoke to two men. On his way back to his Mercedes, he was shot seven times from behind.

Nikolai Radev was dead. Witnesses in the street had seen a car that looked exactly like one belonging to Carl Williams' father. In 2007, Carl Williams

would go to jail for a number of other murders. However, he did a deal with the prosecution that he would plead guilty to those murders if neither he nor his father was tried for Radev's death. Another criminal, a hit man called Andrew 'Benji' Veniamin, might have been one of the killers.

Radev's lifestyle had been good, but he died owing a lot of people money. Police found plenty of expensive goods at his home after his death. However, the money was gone, most probably stolen by fellow criminals. This didn't stop him from being buried in a gold-plated coffin. If Nikolai Radev couldn't have his money any more, nobody else was going to get it.

THE MORAN FAMILY

Imagine what it would be like to be a member of a family whose business was crime.

You might live in a nice house and go to an expensive private school, but you would always have to worry about what might happen to you or your parents.

Of course, you might join the family business. Half-brothers Jason and Mark Moran were happy to go into crime – dealing drugs in their case. It was a dangerous and violent way to live, but they didn't mind. Neither did Lewis, Jason's father and Mark's stepfather.

All three men were to die within a few years of each other, in Melbourne's gangland wars.

In 1999, Jason and Mark met their competition, Carl Williams, in a western suburbs park. They were all in the business of producing 'upper' tablets to be sold at nightclubs and parties. Jason and Mark were annoyed because Williams was selling the pills much cheaper than they were, and because some pills he had sold them had fallen apart. They also said he owed them a lot of money.

Jason wanted to teach Williams a lesson, so he shot him in the stomach. He didn't kill Carl, because that way they'd never get their money.

Carl Williams decided to destroy the whole Moran family and their friends.

Williams couldn't do anything for a while, because he was in remand prison on drug charges, waiting for bail, but he didn't waste his time inside. While waiting, he collected a team of hit men to help him in his plan. When he was released on bail, Jason was in prison, but Mark was a target.

He was shot outside his $1.3 million home in Aberfeldie on 15 June 2000.

Lewis guessed who was responsible for Mark's death. He tried to take out a contract on Carl Williams, but had no luck. No one was going to commit murder for the mere $50,000 he was offering.

Jason knew his life was in danger. He tried not to be too predictable in his movements. For a while,

Williams and his hit team had a hard time keeping track of him. Jason even survived one murder attempt.

But there was one thing he did regularly and it cost his life. He took his children to football training in Essendon every Saturday morning. On 21 June 2003, Jason and his friend Pasquale Barbaro took the children to training for the last time.

Afterwards, a gunman simply leaned into their van parked in the car park of the Cross Keys Hotel and shot both men in front of the children sitting terrified in the back seat.

Jason's children had now lost their father and their uncle and would soon enough lose their grandfather.

Lewis Moran had once been involved in illegal gambling, protection rackets and theft. It was Jason and Mark who introduced him to drug dealing, which paid so well.

Like Jason, he was to die because he had a routine.

Lewis didn't care much any more. Both his boys were gone. Some of his best friends had also been killed in the gangland wars. He knew he was in danger, but it didn't matter to him.

In fact, he had been in remand prison on drugs charges and had fought to get out on bail, even though he was safer in jail than free. The police were trying to protect him by keeping him behind bars, but he wouldn't be protected. Police made his bail conditions changeable so that any gunmen would find him hard to track.

The trouble was, Moran loved his glass of beer. And he had to get it from the same place every day. Everyone knew where to find him from six p.m. onwards: the Brunswick Club bar. On 31 March 2004, two gunmen burst into the pub's front bar and started shooting. Moran tried to escape, but had no chance. With two bullet wounds, he died on the spot.

The Moran men were dead now, but the war continued until 2006, when Carl Williams went to prison for several murders.

MARIO CONDELLO – THE EX-LAWYER

Mario Condello was born in Carlton in 1952, to a hard-working family from the Italian region of Calabria. Mario was given every chance to shine in his family's adopted country. His brother, Enzo, certainly did. Enzo became a well-known playwright.

In fact, Mario did well at first, studying law at Melbourne University and practising law in Carlton afterwards.

But Mario had other plans for his life. In 1982, he was sentenced to six years in jail on fraud and drug-related charges. He was banned from practising law again.

Mario was working for the Calabrian Mafia, importing and distributing drugs in Australia. This job gave him more money and power than working as a lawyer ever could.

Condello knew a lot of people and at one point was running a sort of criminal employment agency. Did you want someone to burn down your business so you could claim insurance? He could arrange it. You needed advice on growing marijuana? He knew just the person to help you! For a price, of course.

He was also a loan shark. Those people who

couldn't persuade banks to lend them money could come to good old Mario. Naturally, they had to be willing to pay huge interest rates. And if you borrowed from Mario, you'd better pay up on time. Mario wouldn't just sell your house. He'd send the boys around to 'talk' to you.

In 1980, the police set up an entire taskforce, Operation Zulu, to investigate what Mario was doing. The taskforce worked for two years and found he was involved in drug trafficking, arson, fraud and one attempted murder.

Police raided the home of a criminal with whom Mario had been in jail and found a list of names and phone numbers. They were all the same as the surname of the detective who had started up the Zulu investigation. Clearly, someone was trying to track down this detective.

After all the jail time he had done, Condello was careful not to be directly involved in crime. He was satisfied to be the one who arranged and financed it. This made it a lot harder to build evidence against him.

Besides, although he was responsible for a lot of violence, someone who had worked with him said he couldn't use a gun and fainted at the sight of blood!

Condello bought a lot of property in Australia and Europe. He owned expensive cars and homes. He gambled at Crown Casino, spending at least $7.5 million a year on his hobby.

And still, he had no day job anyone knew about.

It was because of Mario Condello that police finally managed to arrest the drug dealer Carl Williams without a chance of bail.

Police believed Williams had a contract out on Condello. Mario was a friend of Mick Gatto, who had killed one of Williams' hit men, Andrew Veniamin. Gatto was in prison, but Williams could take his revenge on Condello.

Police, who knew something was going on, were bugging Williams and his hit men. Mostly, this was useless, but there was a breakthrough in May 2004, when two of Williams' hit men were talking in a car they thought was clean. They were discussing a plan to kill Condello while he was walking his dog outside his Brighton home. They didn't know Condello had moved just after Veniamin's death.

It took a while for police to catch them in the attempt. Twice, the hit men slept in. Once, one of them was on a hot date when he was supposed to be committing murder. But on 9 June 2004, the two men were caught.

Williams and his men were charged with conspiracy to kill Condello, but that was all right, because four days later, Mario was arrested for conspiracy to kill Williams and his father, George. Unfortunately for Mario, the 'hit man' to whom he offered $500,000 for the killing was a police informer.

Mario survived until 6 February 2006. After a nice dinner with friends at a Bourke Street restaurant, he left for home. He had a strong security system, but someone followed him into the garage and shot him.

There were 600 mourners at his funeral at St Ignatius Church in Richmond. Most of the mourners, old and young, male and female, were wearing sunglasses, a gangster fashion statement.

According to his family and the priest, Father Norden, Condello 'got religion' during his last year of life, praying daily and carrying a rosary on the night he was shot.

But Father Norden told the congregation, 'Never try revenge.'

DID YOU KNOW...?

Australia's first piece of art was the Charlotte Medal. It was commissioned by the First Fleet ship Charlotte's surgeon and made from a silver kidney dish by convict Thomas Barnett. It is a very beautiful piece of work, with the ship, sun, moon and stars on one side and a description of the voyage on the other. The medal was bought in 2008 by Sydney's National Maritime Museum. Barnett didn't have such a happy ending. On the way to Australia, he continued the forgery for which he'd been transported in the first place, making quarter-dollars to buy goods, through the portholes, from merchants in Rio Di Janeiro. Only a few weeks after arrival in Australia, Thomas stole some food and was executed.

DONNA HAYES AND BENJAMIN JORGENSEN
THE APRIL FOOL'S DAY STUFF-UP

Parents of two and armed-robber wannabes, Donna Hayes and Benjamin Jorgensen, will always have good reason to hate April Fool's day.

The pair hadn't lived together for a while, but when they needed cash badly, they decided to work as a team to raise it.

Benjamin hadn't taken drugs for years, but had gone back to them after a failed relationship had upset him badly. Donna, also a drug user, had used speed to help her get through a long night of housework in 2006. Two days later, she had still had drugs in her blood when she drove 100 km an hour in a 70 km zone. There was an accident and somebody died.

She was out on bail for that charge when the couple received a tip-off. The manager of the Cuckoo, a popular restaurant in Melbourne's Dandenong Ranges, would be carrying over $30,000 in cash after the restaurant closed on Sunday 1 April 2007. This had to be the perfect way to raise the money they wanted so badly!

Benjamin armed himself with a sawn-off shotgun.

Later, he said he hadn't intended to hurt anyone, just frighten his victims. This may be true, but the gun was still loaded. It was going to make trouble for them and send Donna to hospital. Donna took a hammer to use as her weapon. With a third person to drive the getaway car, they went to Olinda, the suburb where the restaurant was located.

After midnight, when the staff members were beginning to leave, they sprang out at the restaurant's manager, Peter Schmidt, who was carrying a black plastic bag.

'Give me the bag or I'll blow your head off!' shouted Benjamin.

'What do you want with the bag?' asked the surprised Peter Schmidt. 'There's only bread rolls in there.'

But he handed over the bag and also didn't think it was safe to argue when Jorgensen demanded his car keys.

That was when things really began to go wrong for the klutzy armed robbers. Jorgensen fumbled with the keys, trying to open the wrong car. His gun went off, but it didn't shoot the robbery victim. It hit Donna, who fell to the ground screaming with pain.

While this was going on, Schmidt and his boss, Horst Lantzsch, ran back into the restaurant, where they called police.

Poor Donna and Benjamin! They had failed to get their money. One of them was injured. And the rolls weren't even fresh! Peter Schmidt had been taking them home to feed his chickens.

Somehow, the failed robbers got back to their car and drove to Donna's home in Belgrave. There, Benjamin asked a friend to take Donna to hospital. If he had taken her himself, perhaps the police would have taken longer to find him, but they caught up with him at the house soon afterwards.

Donna was moved from the William Angliss, a local hospital, to Melbourne's Alfred Hospital, where she was treated, but kept under guard.

Melbourne newspapers, which thought the story was very funny, couldn't agree on where Donna had been injured. Some papers said she'd been shot in the stomach. Others thought the wound was in her hip, or her hip and leg. There was even a suggestion she had been shot in the bum!

Wherever she had been injured, Donna survived and both she and Benjamin went on trial for the attempted robbery. They must have been very embarrassed. Certainly, the court felt that they had both shown remorse for their crime. Benjamin's family said that this was just not the sort of thing that he would normally do.

That didn't stop them from being sentenced to fairly long terms in jail. The judge, who called them fools, took into account their problems and Benjamin's prospects of rehabilitation. Still, Benjamin received a term of seven years, with a minimum of four-and-a-half years before he could apply for parole. Donna's sentence was longer. She would have to spend at least five-and-a-half years of her eight-year sentence in jail.

They would have a long time to cringe with embarrassment over their failed attempt to get the dough!

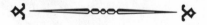

CARL WILLIAMS
DRUG DEALER AND GANGSTER

Happy birthday – bang! Being shot in the stomach isn't a great birthday gift. It was the gift Jason Moran gave Carl Williams on his twenty-ninth birthday in October 1999, when they met to discuss their business differences in a park in Melbourne's western suburbs.

Carl decided to return the favour, with interest. Not only Jason, but also his family and friends would die for this particular birthday present.

For a long time, even police thought that Carl Williams was only working for the family crime business, not running it. He was fat and cheerful-looking. One of his former teachers from Broadmeadows Technical School said he was always half-asleep.

But Carl called himself the Premier, because, he said, he ran the state.

After dropping out of school in Year 11, Carl got a job stacking shelves at a supermarket. He didn't do it for long, though. Working for bookies at the racetrack was more fun.

When he was 24, he was sentenced to ten months in prison for working for drug dealers, but it was reduced to six. The judge thought he was likely to go straight.

Even judges can get it wrong.

By the time he was shot in that park, Carl had a lot of money, a pill-pressing machine, someone to cook the drugs for him and plenty of supporters in the underworld drug industry.

In the world of crime, you don't dob. Carl told police he had been just walking along when he had felt the bullet hit him. No, he didn't know who had done it.

For a while, he and his enemies were popping

in and out of jail, just missing each other. But Carl didn't waste his prison time. While he was in remand prison over drug-manufacturing charges late in 1999, he began to arrange his revenge, discussing his plans with people who later carried out his hits. When he was out on bail, Jason Moran was inside, but that was okay. Mark Moran was still around and Carl could start with him.

Carl shot Mark Moran outside his home on 15 June 2000. It was the only time he actually pulled the trigger himself, but there were at least ten underworld killings which police believe he arranged. He will never be tried for most of them.

In 2001, the Morans plotted to kill Williams at his daughter's christening. Police were informed about it three days before and decided that the best way to protect him was to make sure he was in jail. With the previous charge still hanging over his head, it shouldn't be too hard. An undercover police agent pretended to want to buy drugs from him. He sold them – and found himself back inside.

While Williams was in prison, in September 2001, Jason Moran was released. Police persuaded Jason to take his family out of the country, as his life was in danger. He went, but foolishly returned after only a few months.

Carl Williams and his hit men discussed a number of crazy ideas. The loopiest was to have the hit man dress as a woman and whip a gun out of a pram!

Williams went as far as buying a wig for that, before dropping the plan.

Jason was hard to catch, but finally, they shot him after a children's football clinic in Essendon, in front of his children.

Lewis Moran, Jason's father and Mark's stepfather, was next. He was killed at his favourite pub in March 2004.

Police were frustrated. They believed they knew who was behind so many gangland killings, but couldn't get enough evidence. Carl and his wife, Roberta, knew that their home, cars and phones were bugged. Police listening in to the Williams home complained it was like listening to 24 hours of the Jerry Springer show. What it wasn't, was useful.

Finally, though, they managed to record something that let them arrest Carl, without the possibility of bail. Williams was one of a number of criminals charged with planning to kill Mario Condello. Now there was time to get evidence.

Realising that he might end up spending the rest of his life in prison, Carl did a deal. He pleaded guilty to three counts of murder, provided that a fourth was dropped. His total jail sentence was 35 years.

Mario Condello died anyway, shot in early 2006.

DID YOU KNOW...?

In 2001, British backpackers Peter Falconio and Joanne Lees bought a Kombi van to travel aroundAustralia. Unfortunately, while they were in the Northern Territory, driving down the Stuart Highway, they stopped when Bradley John Murdoch flagged them down, indicating that there was something wrong with the van. Murdoch attacked the tourists. Joanne Lees managed to escape and contact police, starting a major manhunt. Murdoch was caught and convicted, but Peter's body was never found. In 2008, Northern Territory police released the orange van, offering to auction it for Joanne Lees, now back in England, but she asked for it to be destroyed instead, not wanting it to become a horrible relic for someone with weird tastes.

THE ADVENTURES OF
TONY MOKBEL

In August 2001, Antonios Sajih 'Tony' Mokbel was charged with importing millions of dollars worth of pure cocaine, hidden in Mexican statues and candles. The trial was going to take two years to get started and he argued that his businesses would collapse if he had to be in jail, on remand, all that time. Because of this, he was granted bail.

Actually, it took a lot longer than two years. At one point, his bail was withdrawn and he was back in jail. Two drug squad officers involved in his case were arrested themselves. Then he was charged with threatening a prison officer, but the charge was dropped and he was released on bail again in September 2002. A witness against him went overseas after being released on parole. The man promised to come back for the trial, but then demanded $500,000 for his services.

In 2005, Mokbel was charged with inciting others to import drugs. By the time the trial over cocaine importing began, it was February 2006. He offered to plead guilty to trafficking if the importing charge could be dropped. This began to look as if it might happen.

Then the court made a huge mistake and released him on bail again.

Mokbel disappeared.

By the time he was found and arrested in Greece early in 2007, there had been plenty of rumours of where he might be and how he'd escaped. It was only after he was brought back to Australia that the truth came out.

Mokbel had had months to plan out his escape from Australia. He also had plenty of money and friends to help him. While police were searching for him in several countries, Tony Mokbel was living comfortably at a friend's house in the Victorian town of Bonnie Doon.

Another friend, Byron Pantazis, flew to Greece, where he hired some Greek sailors. The sailors flew to Australia, where they bought a 17.3 metre motor yacht from an unsuspecting owner for $350,000. *Edwena* (meaning 'rich friend') was a good yacht. It had sailed around the world before. It was comfortable, but not flashy enough to be noticed by anyone who might be asking questions.

The boat sailed to Newcastle in New South Wales, where it was put on a truck and taken to Fremantle in Western Australia. It was re-fitted along the way and more work was done at the Fremantle Yacht Club. An extra – hidden – cabin was built in what had been storage for the sail, and an extra toilet added.

Now Mokbel left Bonnie Doon and crossed the country in a 4WD. He met the crew between Perth and Geraldton.

On 11 November 2006, *Edwena* sailed from Fremantle. Customs there recorded the departure of three Greek sailors. They didn't find the fourth man, hidden aboard the boat. Nobody paid any attention to the fact that there were four lifejackets when there were supposed to be only three people aboard.

The trip took 40 days and nights, with *Edwena* reaching Greece on Christmas Eve. By that time, Mokbel must have been very happy to be back on land. He was horribly seasick all the way. No doubt, the sea voyage had seemed like a great idea at the time he'd thought of it.

After all that trouble, he was caught in Athens only a few months later, having a cup of hot chocolate at his favourite outdoor café. He was wearing a wig, but that didn't help him much.

It still took nearly a year to get him back to Australia, because he fought it through the Greek courts. He complained that he wouldn't get a fair trial in Australia. He said it was like handing him over to Hitler.

But when he finally did come home in May 2008, he returned in first-class comfort. The airlines refused to carry him and his minders, so a private plane had to be chartered to get him back.

As he had been tried and convicted in his absence, and there would be more charges to come, it will probably be his last taste of first-class living for quite a while.

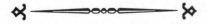

BIBLIOGRAPHY

If you're a member of a public library, just use your membership card to log into the library's website and you can use the online resources, including encyclopaedias. I did. I also used a lot of newspapers on the Internet, but there's nothing like checking out newspapers as they come out!

I used about a million books, newspapers and websites to look up the information for this book. Here are a few you might like:

For children:

Tucker, Alan: *Iron in the Blood: Convicts and Commandants in Colonial Australia*. Norwood, SA: Omnibus, 2002.

Sharpe, Alan: *The Illustrated Book of Infamous Australian Crimes*. Milson's Point: Brolga, 1982.

Gard, Stephen: *The Bushrangers (Settling Australia)*. South Yarra, Macmillan, 1998.

For adults:

Morton, James, Lobez, Susanna: *Gangland Australia*. Carlton, Melbourne University Press, 2007.

Peters, Allan L, *True and Infamous Crimes of Australia and New Zealand*. Seaford, Bas Publishing.

Roberts, Murray Beresford: *A King of Con Men*. Auckland: Hodder and Stoughton, c 1975.

Silvester, John & Rule, Andrew: *Gotcha: How Australia's Baddest Crooks Copped Their Right Whack*. Camberwell, Victoria: Floradale Productions, Sly Ink, 2005.

Silvester, John & Rule, Andrew: *Underbelly: The Gangland War*. Camberwell, Victoria: Floradale Productions, Sly Ink, 2008.

Taylor, Paul: *Australian Ripping Yarns: Cannibal Convicts, Macabre Murders, Wanton Women and Living Legends*. Rowville, Victoria: Five Mile Press, 2004.

Websites:

Australian Dictionary of Biography Online Edition: www.adb.online.anu.edu.au/adbonline.htm

Melbourne Crime (really good for the gangland wars): www.melbournecrime.bizhosting.com/index.html

Wikipedia: www.wikipedia.org

INDEX

THANK YOU

First, Paul Collins of Ford Street Publishing, who believed I could write this book, and to Saralinda Turner, for looking up a lot of gruesome stories so she could edit it.

Grant Gittus and Louise Prout made this book look terrific – much appreciated!

Many thanks to Kerry Greenwood and Chris Wheat, who helped me out when I was trying to find stories that didn't involve serial killers!

Bouquets to Bart Rutherford O'Connor and teachers at his school who checked the cover with students – and to students and staff at Sunshine College West Campus who listened patiently to bits from the book and commented on the cover.

Finally, I want to thank the gang at the Presse Café in Elwood, where I wrote a lot of this book, for keeping the tea and muffins coming and showing such interest.

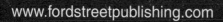